Being the Change

Being the Change

In the Footsteps of the Mahatma

Ashutosh Salil
Barkha Mathur

HarperCollins *Publishers* India

First published in India by HarperCollins *Publishers* 2022
4th Floor, Tower A, Building No. 10, Phase II, DLF Cyber City,
Gurugram, Haryana –122002
www.harpercollins.co.in

2 4 6 8 10 9 7 5 3 1

P-ISBN: 978-93-5629-198-0
E-ISBN: 978-93-5629-199-7

Typeset in 11.5/16 Bembo Std
Manipal Technology Ltd, Manipal

Printed and bound at
Thomson Press (India) Ltd

To

My lovely parents Meena and Vijay—Salil

My mother Usha, who taught me to write—Barkha

Contents

Introduction

WHY WE WROTE THIS BOOK

We are both in professions of service to people, albeit in our own ways—one of us is a bureaucrat and the other a journalist. For the both of us, each day brings a new blur of people and faces we meet, work with and for.

Among the many, many people we regularly come across, the ones that have stayed on in our minds are not the rich and the powerful, or even the talented or the successful. The ones that have stayed on in our consciousness, invariably, are the ones doing selfless work—those working for the uplift of others.

We are not talking of social work. We are talking about being the change we want to see in the world. Of making one's life one's message—the teachings of Mahatma Gandhi that are increasingly becoming relics in the maddening machinery of modern life.

One of us—the bureaucrat—felt the need to document the lives of a few such extraordinary individuals. The other—the journalist—has covered most of them in the course of her work spanning two decades. Both of us decided to put together a book on the lives and works of some such people in Vidarbha, largely the eastern region of Maharashtra—because it is our own *karmabhoomi* (place of work), because it is also fertile ground for social movements and has a deep connection with Mahatma Gandhi.

As we discussed the project, it became clear that both of us had the same objective—we have both always felt that the stories of these men and women needed to travel beyond the geographical boundaries of where they live and work.

After a couple of e-mail exchanges, we picked seven such stories from a formidable list of eleven. The selections were made on the basis of the impact of their work, and the lives these individuals had been able to touch and change for the better.

Between July and November 2019, we travelled across Vidarbha to meet our heroes—and sheroes—and hear their stories. The process of putting the material together for the book was fulfilling. It gave us a sense of what selfless service really means—it helped us understand how much can be achieved through perseverance and resilience, and most importantly, it reaffirmed how timeless and perennial Bapu's teachings are.

Besides bringing out the stories of service to mankind, the purpose of this book is also to underline how relevant Mahatma Gandhi and his teachings remain even in the new millennium. How, by following his path, ordinary people can still make a difference to the lives of those who do not get our attention.

We sincerely hope that the book will motivate many others to reach out to the less-privileged and swivel the spotlight to the noble work being done in the remote areas of Vidarbha and elsewhere in India.

Ashutosh Salil
Barkha Mathur

Bandu Dhotre

THE GREEN WARRIOR OF CHANDRAPUR

The Indian Forest Service officer was flabbergasted. He did not have time for sermons from a *sarp mitra,* the name given by the Maharashtra forest department to volunteers who rescue snakes. 'How does this concern you? Mind your own business,' the officer snapped at the tall young man in front of him. The official's curtness was understandable. The Ministry of Coal, Government of India, had, in November 2007, allotted a mining lease for 1,750 hectares of land in Lohara, a village in Maharashtra's Chandrapur district. Who was this man, who seemed neither well off nor very educated, to poke his nose into such important things?

What the official did not know, however, was that Bandu Dhotre, who had asked about the coal mining project and its environmental impact, did not fit the mould of a not-very-educated ordinary man—even though he lived in a shanty in the Chandrapur district headquarters, was not even a graduate, and even though he indeed was a sarp mitra, literally meaning a friend of snakes. But what the officer didn't know was that he also ran an organization called Eco-Pro.

The village where the coal mine was to come up was close to the buffer zone of the Tadoba–Andhari Tiger Reserve, a national park in Maharashtra that is part of central India's big-cat corridor through Madhya Pradesh, Chhattisgarh and Telangana. The coal blocks, which were close to the proposed buffer zone of the reserve, had been allotted for the Tiroda power plant, which was to be located around 250 kilometres away in the Gondia district of Maharashtra's eastern Vidarbha region. A friend of Bandu's, who worked for an advocate, had come to know of this through his employer. 'I think your friend Bandu should take up the issue,' the lawyer had told his employee.

In 2009, Bandu Dhotre had become a household name in Chandrapur as a warrior for the environment when his organization, Eco-Pro, had resurrected the city's landmark water body by clearing it of the choking grip of water hyacinths.

The news of the coal block allocation had alarmed Bandu. He was appalled that thousands of trees would be felled for mining. That the lush, pristine forests would be denuded. That the hills that were home to tigers, leopards, sloth bears, wild boars, dholes (Indian wild dogs), many kinds of deer, thousands of birds and other endangered animals would be dug up to extricate coal. Bandu, through Eco-Pro, had been trying so hard to create awareness about how the jungles should be protected.

Thus, he had walked into the office of the deputy conservator of forests and introduced himself as a sarp mitra, sending a request for a meeting through a peon. The high-ranking officer, however, was in no mood to be lectured on ecological conservation and wildlife protection by a semi-literate snake charmer.

The official's apathy filled Bandu with a quiet rage. He would risk his life to save every snake in Chandrapur, if he had to. Here, a huge habitat for wildlife was about to be destroyed and the officer was asking how it concerned him? He walked out of the government office with a steady determination building in him. It was like he was a child again with only one aim in life—which, as a child, was to join the Indian Army.

~

Every year during the nine days of Chaitra Navratri, in March–April, there is a *jatra,* a holy congregation, at the Mahakali temple in Chandrapur, thronged by thousands of devotees from across Maharashtra, Madhya Pradesh, Telangana and Chhattisgarh. The area around the temple dons a festive look at this time. Shops spring up, selling everything from vermilion and other offerings to the deity to eatables and knick-knacks. Bandu's father, Sitaram Dhotre, a small shopkeeper, sold groceries in the main market of Chandrapur. During the jatra, Sitaram would shift his business closer to the temple in the hope of cashing in on the pilgrim rush. Often accompanying him would be the eldest of his four sons, Bandu, who would help him put up mounds of powdered spices and rows of neatly segregated whole ones. Father and son would then wait for buyers to come.

The young boy, mostly to kill boredom, would observe the groups of devotees as they passed, singing devotional songs and swaying in a trance. Close to their stall sat an astrologer. With a caged parrot, a pack of cards spread out on a plastic sheet and an almanac in hand, he would painstakingly set a trap for passers-by wanting a peek into their future. The thirteen-year-old Bandu would watch with interest as the young and the old alike stopped by to know what the cards foretold. One day, he borrowed a rupee from his father and approached the pandit. 'Can you tell me what my future will be?' he said hesitantly, as if fearing what the cards might hold for him. Sizing up the lanky lad, the fortune teller studied the lines on his palm for a while before declaring, 'You are destined to be an officer in the Indian Army.'

That lit a spark in Bandu's heart and gave him a mission in life. Now that the all-knowing clairvoyant had said so, the Class VII student felt that his joining the army was a certainty. He craved for the adventure of a soldier's life and to be looked up to as a protector of the land. His entire world revolved around this dream.

A year later, when he was in Class VIII, Bandu learnt that the National Cadet Corps (NCC) could give him a much-needed shortcut to reach his goal. All he had to do was get selected, for which he would have to clear the certificate course for students of classes VIII and IX. Tall boys who could march with precision had a bright chance of being selected, he was told.

On the day of the selection parade, Bandu reached the school ground excited but unprepared. The shirt he was wearing was torn at the ends and two buttons were missing. It was a windy day. The shirt, with its loose ends, flapped in the breeze and Bandu had to constantly use one hand to keep it in place. He kept falling out of step and his hands were not in sync as he struggled with the unruly shirt. 'You cannot march,' the instructor barked as he pulled Bandu out of the line. The young boy was devastated—his dream lay tattered like his shirt.

At home, too, the fabric of Bandu's life was falling apart. His father had left them to live with another woman. Sitaram would visit the family sometimes, but paid little attention to how his wife, four sons and daughter were surviving. Bandu's mother, Suman, was left alone to fend for the family. She tried to sell spices by the roadside like her husband, but the money was never enough. Desperate, she joined her sister, who carried vegetables from a farm to the market. Each basket the women carried on their heads would fetch them around Rs 3. The sisters made five to six such rounds, walking around 6 kilometres every day to make about Rs 30 collectively.

Bandu, too, would ferry the load after school to augment the income. At the end of each day, the two women and the boy would walk home. On their way was a grocery store, where a mishmash of grains that had spilled out of their respective bags and got mixed up during the day's business was sold at Rs 2.5 per kilo. Sometimes they would buy a kilo or two. At home, the three of them would separate the dal from the rice and spices, and a meal would be prepared.

Even in the midst of such despair, Bandu held on to his dream of joining the army. He came to know about a month-long course conducted by the Hanuman Vyayam Prasarak Mandal in Amravati, some 200 kilometres away, which had quite a history. It was set up in 1914 by Ambadaspant Vaidya, who wanted to join the army, but could not make it. It was initially a wrestling club, a *vyayam shala* that would train youth in the Indian tradition of physical fitness. Freedom fighters such as Shivaram Rajguru and Chandra Shekhar Azad had stayed there, hiding from the British colonial police. Legendary figures of Indian history, such as Mahatma Gandhi, Motilal Nehru, Rajendra Prasad and Subhas Chandra Bose, had also visited the vyayam shala. According to Madhuri Vaidya Chainke, secretary of the mandal, the centre had sent participants to the 1936 Berlin Olympics, where they had performed Indian sports such as malkambh, kabaddi and kho-kho, and been given a letter of appreciation by Adolf Hitler that is still displayed at the administrative office. The institution had, in 1939, set up a civil defence force under which a pre-military camp was organized every year in May and June for boys and girls.

Bandu wanted to go to Amravati to train at the camp, which would serve as a stepping stone to the senior wing of the NCC, but he knew his mother could not afford to send him. She did not have the money, and his leaving would mean that the small amount he was being able to pitch in would also be lost. In desperation, Bandu approached his father. Despite living away from his family, Sitaram still cared for his son and believed in his dream of joining the army. With his father's help, Bandu enrolled on the course in Amravati.

The immediate goal was to make it to the senior wing of the NCC and eventually clear the C certificate course with an A or a B grade at the graduation level. This would get him an interview with the Services Selection Board (SSB) of the Indian Army without having to clear the written exam. Bandu dived into the rigours of training in Amravati. When he joined junior college in Class XI, he was prepared for the NCC selection drill. His confidence zoomed when he was selected to lead the parade as a guide in a school event, but that was as far as he would go. Since the C certificate was a three-year course, only students who had enrolled for graduation were selected. Bandu still believed in his dream, but the setbacks were making him restless.

He could finally join the NCC when he entered college in the first year of his BA. The NCC organizes multiple camps throughout graduate studies. There is the prestigious Republic Day camp, for which candidates are selected from across the country. It is from among these candidates that the NCC contingent for the Republic Day parade in New Delhi is chosen.

To get direct entry into the army, it is mandatory to clear the C certificate course with an A or a B grade. For that, it is compulsory to attend one Annual Training Camp and, in addition to it, one of the several others, including the Republic Day camp. Bandu, for once, decided not to punch above his weight. He skipped the trials for the Republic Day camp. He knew that his lack of exposure and grooming would come in the way. Bandu was selected for the Annual Training Camp, but the wind did him in there too. He cleared three levels but lost out in the firing round. When he took the shot, a slight breeze moved the target pinned on the board.

'You have missed the mark very narrowly,' the officer told Bandu. The pellet fired from Bandu's rifle had missed the target and bored through the heart of the only dream he had nurtured since he was thirteen years old. He got a C grade in the C certificate course. Bandu was so upset that he did not take his final-year graduation exams. He slipped into an abyss of depression. For the next six months he roamed around Chandrapur, listless and devoid of the will to bring his life back on track.

~

The Bandu Dhotre who walked out of the office of the deputy conservator of forests angry about the allocation of the mining licence was, however, not the same lost teenager. He had, by then, fought many battles. Every time he had been laid low by life, he had fought to get back up. And this Bandu Dhotre had found his raison d'être—activism, fighting for the greater good.

It was almost as if Bandu's life had been a preparation for this goal. Growing up, he was deeply taken in by the life stories of two men from his school history books—the warrior king Chhatrapati Shivaji Maharaj and the apostle of non-violence, Mahatma Gandhi.

When fate had shut the doors to the army for Bandu, it had opened up a complex detour to activism and fighting for what is right. The path of Gandhi.

Around the year 1999, Bandu, then twenty years old, began to pick up the pieces of his life. He started examining his options for employment. A government job was ruled out as he had not completed his graduation. The easiest opportunity was taking up what is called network marketing—direct sales of goods and services. Bandu had some natural advantages in this. He cut an imposing figure at around 6 feet tall and had a soldier's demeanour. He was articulate but soft-spoken, and he could push a product. So he started selling utility items to the people of Chandrapur. He also began to take a keen interest in the happenings in his neighbourhood to be able to expand his network. The youth association in his locality would set up pandals—temporary structures made of bamboo and canvas—for the festivals celebrating Lord Ganesha and Goddess Durga. Putting to use his newly discovered organizational capabilities and networking skills, Bandu became the go-to person for everyone involved in these festivities.

It was at one such gathering that he met a young girl named Yojana. She had come to Chandrapur from Amravati and lived with her maternal uncle. Yojana's mother had moved in with her brother and taken up work as a domestic help when the condition of Yojana's father, who suffered from mental health issues, worsened. As they lived in the same neighbourhood, Yojana and Bandu would chat when they ran into each other.

The friendship was also born out of need. She was in Class XII, and Bandu began to help with her stationery and books. Gradually, the two fell in love. They worked together with the youth associations, organizing events. Their romance blossomed over the next five years, and finally they decided to tie the knot. Yojana's uncle opposed the relationship, citing Bandu's caste—he was a Lohar and she a Dhobi—and lack of education, but love triumphed and the two got married in 2004.

Marriage brought some joy to Bandu's life, but it did not stop his streak of bad luck. It now struck at his workplace.

Bandu realized that his bosses were planning to abscond with the money that agents such as him had collected through the sales of products and memberships. This troubled him greatly. 'Ultimately, it will be the people of my city, whom I have enrolled as members, who will end up being duped,' he told Yojana. He decided to blow the whistle by calling up the head office of the company in Mumbai. 'I think something very fishy is brewing here at the Chandrapur office,' he informed the management's top brass. Immediately after his complaint, the local office in Chandrapur was shut down. Bandu was left jobless.

Desperation filled him once again. How would he support his family? How would he pay back those who formed his network marketing chain? Revulsion over his bosses' dishonesty and a feeling of being cheated swamped him. Filled with rage, he also realized something else—that making money was not what he enjoyed, that it was not enough to motivate him.

He decided to serve his city, in whatever way he could. It would, in a way, be his penance for unknowingly luring the people of his city into being part of dubious schemes.

~

Chandrapur, located in the extreme east of Maharashtra, was a major factor in the transformation of Bandu Dhotre. The district, one of eleven in Vidarbha, has vast tracts of coal mines, a paper mill and cement factories. Nearly 40 per cent of Chandrapur is also under lush forest cover, home to rich and thriving wildlife. The district headquarters has heritage structures—temples and fort walls more than 500 years old—giving it a distinct character.

Bandu realized that what affected the lives of people in Chandrapur most were environmental issues, such as frequent flooding during monsoons, man-animal conflict, and various civic and social problems. His training in disaster management, civil defence and rescue management at the Hanuman Vyayam Prasarak Mandal and the NCC could help him do something good for the city. He could not guard the borders of the country, but he could defend it internally from calamities.

By 2005, Bandu, then twenty-six years old, managed to gather a bunch of young, energetic volunteers ready to rise to the occasion whenever Chandrapur needed them. He schooled them in disaster management through physical training. His group, which he named Nagar Saurakshak Dal, started helping with rescue work during floods and other emergencies.

One day, a snake was spotted in a neighbour's home. It was a cobra—one of the 'big four' venomous snake species that causes probably the most number of human deaths in the Indian subcontinent. The practice is to contact the forest department when a snake is found. They sometimes inform a sarp mitra to do the job and the custom is to pay him Rs 100 for it. The payment is made by the people and not the forest department. Bandu realized that people living in slums could barely afford to pay Rs 100 to catch a snake. They would rather kill it. Bandu decided to become a sarp mitra and do it for free. This would be his contribution towards his people, as well as to wild animals.

There was also the adrenaline boost of risk and adventure in the job that attracted him. But first he had to know how to catch a snake. So Bandu trained under a professional snake charmer to learn the skill.

He began to get calls from across Chandrapur, because he was getting rid of snakes for free. By the time a year rolled by, he was flooded with so many requests to capture snakes that he realized he could not do it alone. It was time to raise a group of volunteers to help him. He conducted a workshop on the art of catching snakes. This made him quite popular around the city.

Perhaps a testament to his love for the regimented life of the army, he decided to give his work an organizational structure. The same year, in 2006, he formed Eco-Pro, a bunch of people dedicated to environmental and wildlife protection. He even designed a uniform for Eco-Pro. 'I selected the trouser cloth used for army fatigues, which speaks of battles and challenges; the T-shirt is white as it symbolizes peaceful ways of protest and sacrifices that have to be made. The touch of green on the collar and sleeves of the T-shirt shows that we work for the protection of the environment,' he says.

One of the most prominent landmarks of Chandrapur is the more-than-500-year-old Ramala Talao, a water body built by the Gond tribal king Khandkya Ballal Shah, who ruled from the neighbouring town of Ballarshah. When he started building the city of Chandrapur, the king ordered that an 11-kilometre-long outer wall be built. The Ramala lake was also constructed at that time, and runs along the north-east section of the wall. The next Gond king, Ram Shah, renovated and repaired the lake, and constructed stone ghats there. The water body was named after him. Cut to 2009 and the Ramala Talao was covered with water hyacinth, an invasive, fast-growing plant species that chokes water bodies by consuming the dissolved oxygen in water, which kills aquatic life. Eco-Pro dived into the work of resuscitating the lake. Bandu's band began to enlist the help of volunteers. Young and old, including from other established local organizations, joined the movement to clean the lake. The effort turned into a big campaign and Bandu became something of a local hero.

The coal block allocation happened soon after that—at a time that Bandu was ready for bigger battles.

~

Stung by the forest official's snub, Bandu asked for information about the coal block under the then-three-year-old Right to Information Act. For a month, he immersed himself in research, going through the legalese and intricacies of government policy.

He then took the help of his friends in the media—by now he was a known name in Chandrapur—to draft a letter stating why the coal block allocation should be cancelled. He delivered the letter to the district collector, forest officers and political leaders.

Bandu began to oppose the coal block allocation at the public hearings that were held as part of the due process. Through the year 2008, he fought to prevent mining activities in the region. Initially, local politicians supported him. Gradually, however, the enthusiasm among most people and the will to fight began to wilt, giving way to an acceptance that the mining would begin. But Bandu was not deterred—he held on to hope.

There were many environmental organizations opposing the allocation. He realized he needed to up the ante and take his fight to the doorstep of the government. The Maharashtra state legislature holds its fortnight-long winter session in Nagpur, 150 kilometres from Chandrapur, in December. As the entire state administration shifts from Mumbai, many agitations and protests are usually organized to catch the attention of the lawmakers.

Bandu, too, arrived in Nagpur in December 2008 to protest against the allotment of mining rights. He sat on a fast in the area marked for agitators outside the legislature building. The seriousness of the issue and his firm resolve managed to catch the attention of the government. On the eighth day of his fast, the state forest minister met him and promised to look into the coal block allocation. Soon, a committee to find methods to reduce the damage caused by mining was formed. Bandu was appointed as one of its members. But he would have none of it. He quit the panel, saying, 'I am fighting to get the mining orders quashed. Why would I look for ways to reduce the damage caused by mining?'

His anger was justified. The area had been declared a critical tiger habitat. Mining would restrict the movement of the already dwindling number of big cats and other animals, and endanger their very existence. Bandu returned to Chandrapur, once again dejected and disappointed. But he was far too determined to give up. He vowed to fight on, this time in a more planned manner—by involving other environmental agencies.

Bandu's marketing experience had taught him that if he wanted to get the entire district headquarters involved in the agitation, he had to create and keep up the buzz. It was important that he be able to connect with the people and that they, too, join the agitation. Bandu went on an indefinite fast from 20 July 2009.

While he sat on the fast, his volunteers organized events such as a *sadbuddhi mahayagna* (prayers for good sense to prevail), a *mundan andolan* (tonsuring of the head, like it is done when one loses a parent), and performing the 'last rites' of animals that would perish due to the mining activities. Bandu's band also fanned out, explaining the toll mining would take on the jungles and the city. The local media covered the agitation in detail. It caught the attention of the city folk and people came out in support.

On the ninth day of the fast, a call was sounded for a Chandrapur bandh, a shutdown in protest. The call resonated throughout the city. Voluntarily, shops, organizations and private offices pulled down their shutters. It was a historic moment for Chandrapur, and a big validation for Bandu and his agitation. Anti-mining sentiment was raging in the city and the district. Bandu had gone without food and water for eight days, and his condition was critical. Fearing for his life, the district administration forcibly shifted him to a hospital, where he was put in the Intensive Care Unit. But he continued his fast.

News of the agitation and support for it reached New Delhi. Jairam Ramesh, who was India's environment minister then, wrote to Bandu promising to look into the matter, but on condition that Bandu first end his fast. Not convinced by the platitudes, Bandu continued his agitation.

On the thirteenth day of his fast, he got a call from Jairam Ramesh. The minister promised to visit Chandrapur to take stock of the ground realities. 'But you have to first end your fast,' he again told Bandu. Convinced that something would be done this time, Bandu relented.

The minister did visit Chandrapur. A first-hand evaluation of the situation gave Jairam Ramesh better insight into the issue and the damage that mining would cause. The allocation was stalled. Chandrapur erupted in joy. Bandu had achieved an epic victory. A slum dweller had stopped the government from carrying out mining in the environmentally sensitive area. Later, in February 2014, the coal block allotment was cancelled.

~

All this while, as Bandu was fighting for social causes and becoming a household name in Chandrapur, his young wife was braving her battles alone.

The five years of courtship had put stars in Yojana's eyes. She was a vulnerable young girl when she had met Bandu. He was her knight in shining armour, with his confidence in himself and the way he spoke about issues of larger concern. He was her idol. She had felt he was different. She still believes that.

But when Yojana arrived to live at her in-laws' place, the misty visions of love were replaced by the miasma of reality. Her uncle was a man of average means, but she had lacked nothing in his home. Her in-laws' place was a shanty in which she and her husband had to share two tiny rooms with six other people—Bandu's three brothers, his parents (Sitaram had returned to his first wife by now) and an aunt. There was neither electricity nor cooking gas. Water had to be drawn from a well outside. Food was cooked on firewood. Yojana had dreamt of a room for herself in her new home. But here she could not claim even a corner as her own space.

Lack of privacy, however, was hardly the problem. Bandu would be out of the house most of the time, busy with his social work. The young bride would busy herself with household chores and the long wait for her husband to return home.

Yojana and Bandu still live in the same house—which they plan to change soon—and life has not changed much. Still, a shudder runs down her spine when she recalls the early days of her marriage. There was hardly anything to eat most of the time. Her father-in-law was still running the small grocery business. Food would be cooked in the house only when Sitaram returned at night after closing the shop. He would bring the groceries and provisions to prepare the meal. Yojana would start cooking around 8 p.m., serve the family and then wait for her husband to return so that the two of them could share the meal.

After a year of marriage, Yojana gave birth to a son. The couple named him Chitraksh. Bandu's social work was not paying him anything, but he was adamant that he would not do anything else. So Yojana was forced to live with Bandu's parents. Taking care of her son and doing her duties for the family gave Yojana no time or opportunity to look for a job. She would wonder why her husband could not be like the many other volunteers of Eco-Pro. 'There are so many people who work with you but also have jobs,' she would tell him. 'They are also doing social work but they are making sure they provide for their wife and children too.'

Bandu works part-time as an agent with Life Insurance Corporation of India. He admits that with his marketing skills, he can expand his business. But he feels that it would hinder his social service. 'I work for people and take up causes that concern them,' he says. 'It would be ridiculous if I were to start selling them insurance policies.'

As Eco-Pro moved from strength to strength, the only joyous moment in Yojana's life was the birth of her second son, Rudraksh, in 2008. The family's poverty meant her life was mostly filled with squabbles and desperation. Whatever money Bandu earned was not sufficient for his own expenses. He could barely look after the needs of his family. For Yojana, life was a daily battle. 'It is a continuous struggle to meet the needs of two growing boys.

I don't give any attention to my personal requirements as I have understood that there will never be any money for myself,' she would often tell her husband. For Bandu, work also became an escape. The agitations outside were easier to handle than those inside his home. There was enough to keep Bandu away from home most of the time.

Three months after the mining-licence agitation, in December 2009, he once again sat on a fast to draw attention to the air pollution in Chandrapur caused by the open loading and unloading of iron ore and cement on railway wagons. The dust generated, carried across the city by the wind, was causing acute respiratory problems in the people. Bandu's fast pushed the authorities to act. Within eight days of the agitation, Central Railways stopped the activity. Eco-Pro also forced a ban on the use of kerosene as fuel by autorickshaw drivers. The agitations did not just help Chandrapur, which is among India's most polluted cities and industrial areas, but also brought an awakening among the people about the need to protect the environment.

Although Eco-Pro was associated with wildlife and environment-related causes, Bandu knew that he had to widen his reach to make his organization more relevant. Even as he rescued leopards and tigers, he understood that there was a need to take up social and civic causes that touched the everyday lives of people in the city. He soon found one such cause.

The Babupeth railway crossing in Chandrapur is considered one of the busiest in Maharashtra. Nearly one-third of the city's population has to cross it every day to go to work, school, markets or hospitals. The wait at the crossing sparks massive traffic snarls. Ambulances carrying heart-attack patients had to wait endlessly at the crossing and would then get caught in traffic once the gate opened. There had been several instances of delay and even death because of this until 2009. There was even a woman who had had to deliver both her children at the Babupeth railway crossing because she couldn't get to the hospital on time. An overbridge was the crying need. Bandu and his team began to drum up support for it.

Eco-Pro volunteers held a series of meetings in the city's public spaces, persuading people to join the cause. It was decided that on 4 February 2010, they would march to the district collector's office to present their demand. Bandu and his volunteers reached the starting venue at 10 a.m. Half an hour later, just a handful of people had gathered, and even at 11 a.m. it was a thin crowd. The months spent building up support seemed to have been for nothing. Bandu, however, was not deterred. He decided to proceed with the march. As he and his group of volunteers began walking to the district collector's office, people came out and joined them from all directions. Many were carrying placards depicting scenes of distress and hardships near the railway crossing.

'It was like you see in the movies,' recalls Bandu. 'It became the biggest procession the city had ever seen.' The authorities accepted the demand for an overbridge, even though construction finally began many years later, in 2019.

Bandu did not abandon green causes. He had been working closely with forest guards, foresters and forest department officials right up to the rank of chief conservator of forests and principal chief conservator of forests. He had learnt a lot about wildlife protection policies and the gaps in their implementation. In 2011–12, Bandu launched an agitation for better tiger protection, in which he made sixteen demands. These included declaring Chandrapur a 'tiger district' with systems in place for the protection of the big cats outside the core area of national parks, methods of preventing man-animal conflict, setting up anti-poaching patrols and removing the Forest Development Corporation of Maharashtra Limited (FDCM) from Chandrapur.

The corporation was set up to monetize 'degraded forests' by clearing them, and planting teak, sal and other trees that can be sold as forest produce. According to Bandu, the corporation was pulling down jungles and planting trees there, and this was reducing the area reserved for tigers. Bandu wanted a larger expanse of the forest area to be under the territorial forest as it would ensure greater wildlife protection. In July 2013, Bandu sat on a fast for eleven days in Nagpur, and the state government accepted all his demands, except the one that involved having the FDCM removed. But they assured him that FDCM would also work for wildlife protection. Bandu was in the ICU when his delegation held a meeting with the government and accepted the decision.

~

Despite the success and popularity of Eco-Pro in Chandrapur, a feeling of restlessness was gnawing at Bandu—and it had nothing to do with the sufferings of his family. It was the period from 2011 to 2014, when Anna Hazare, another Gandhian activist, had grabbed India's attention. Bandu was reading about the feats of Hazare and how he had brought change in his village, Ralegaon Siddhi, in western Maharashtra. A massive tree-planting drive and measures to retain rainwater had raised the water table there, making it possible for farmers to sow multiple crops in a year. The model was also followed by Hiware Bazar in the drought-prone Ahmednagar district of Maharashtra and Patoda village on the outskirts of Aurangabad. Hazare and the sarpanch of the other two villages had been able to change the fortunes of these villages.

Bandu knew the work he was doing in Chandrapur was equally substantial but it did not attract national attention. He wanted his organization to make waves on a pan-India level.

As luck would have it, in 2015 India's Ministry of Youth Affairs and Sports conferred a National Award for Community Service on Bandu Dhotre. When he travelled to Guwahati in Assam to receive the award, Bandu met other winners from across the country. He learnt about their work and found that what he had been doing in Chandrapur measured up to the achievements of others. He realized that just doing good work was not enough—it was important to send the message out too. 'Think globally and act locally' was the mantra he brought back with him to Chandrapur.

A year earlier, in 2014, India's new Prime Minister, Narendra Modi, had launched the Swachh Bharat Abhiyan—a mission for a clean and hygienic nation. Bandu would often get invites from various organizations taking up activities under the mission. He was deeply disappointed that most of these events were merely photo opportunities. 'Symbolically holding a broom or just sweeping the road or the lane near one's house is not how India will become clean,' he thought.

Bandu had read that both Gandhi and the social reformer-saint Sant Gadge Maharaj had spent time in Chandrapur. Both had highlighted service through cleanliness. Bandu looked around for the right initiative to take up under the Swachh Bharat Abhiyan. His attention fell on the Chanda fort, also in Chandrapur.

The fort was built by the Gond king Khandkya Ballal Shah, who ruled between 1470 and 1495. It took six generations and 125 years for the fort walls to be built. The palaces were located within its walls and later served as jails. By 2016, the fort was falling apart. The walls were crumbling at many places and in many others were buried under huge dumps of garbage. Trees were growing on the thirty-nine ramparts, their roots boring through the structure, opening up massive cracks. Snakes and scorpions crawled in the many crevices. It was like a jungle. Adding to the problems of cleaning and maintaining the structure were the squatters who had built shanties along the fort's walls.

Bandu and Eco-Pro launched a mammoth cleanliness drive for the fort from 1 March 2017, after taking permission from the authorities. A ten-member team, armed with brooms, machetes, chainsaws and rock-climbing equipment, began the task of cleaning the Chanda fort—the Chandrapur Killa Swachhata Abhiyan.

It was a self-driven initiative. Nobody had asked them to do this. It took the city three months to notice the work Bandu and his team were doing. Then, everyone from students to government employees, shopkeepers, autorickshaw drivers and even doctors began to join in. On Sundays and other holidays, hordes of volunteers would reach the area and help clean the Chanda fort.

The district administration, too, pitched in. Notices were issued to people who had encroached upon the space near the fort wall. Some of the squatters, however, moved out on their own because they realized the importance of the work being done. Eco-Pro, with its simple initiative, had created a sense of pride among the people for their city and its heritage structures. After 200 days, Bandu and his volunteers had been able to clean most of the fort. Prime Minister Modi made mention of the work done by them in his weekly radio broadcast, *Mann Ki Baat*. Bandu became the local hero who had gone national. The clean-up of the fort was completed by January 2021.

The goodwill that Eco-Pro has earned in the city over the years has yielded results. In 2018, the organization was gifted a spacious office opposite Ramala Talao. A supporter pays the rent. The office is lined with shelves that display the awards and appreciations Eco-Pro and its founder have received. Everything that the well-furnished office has—from furniture to stationery, from the computers to the ten newspapers that arrive every day—are paid for by ordinary men and women from Chandrapur, who believe in the causes that the organization takes up. Funds from politicians or big companies are declined. Eco-Pro does not work for money or take up projects financed by others.

'If I start taking funds, it will limit the ability of my organization to raise issues of public interest, since then I may be beholden to corporate donors,' Bandu says. The issues that Eco Pro-takes up are of public interest and all he does is mobilize support for them, he insists.

Bandu's battles have been selfless, and the people of Chandrapur have acknowledged this. Since there is no hidden agenda or ambition behind his actions, there is always an outpouring of support for him. He also believes that most bureaucrats are considerate and extend help for good causes. The government officers, he says, are willing to go the extra mile if the movement is for the greater good. In fact, he takes them into confidence before launching any agitation.

In 2008, during the protest against the coal-block allocation, when Bandu wanted eyeballs for his demonstration, he had thought of doing it à la Dharmendra in the epic Seventies' Bollywood blockbuster *Sholay*. 'I asked the deputy superintendent of police at Chandrapur what would happen if I climbed a tower to register my protest. He told me that it would not be proper and that I could get arrested,' Bandu recalls. He abandoned the idea. His organization has been careful not to break the rules.

~

'When the sun shines on one side, the other side falls under a shadow,' Bandu says. This is definitely true of his public and private life. Yojana and Bandu's reality has not changed, even though everyone in the city knows Bandu Dhotre and Eco-Pro. Bandu has succeeded in what he had set out to achieve—be a real-life hero people look up to—but he often feels that he has failed badly as a son, a husband and a father.

'I wanted to be in the army, and my father, in spite of everything else he did, helped me and supported me financially, as somewhere along the way it had become his dream too. But I could not fulfil it,' Bandu rues. As he does not have a steady income, his father still supports him.

Bandu's two young sons, Chitraksh and Rudraksh, struggle to reconcile their father's successful public life with his harsh personal life. Getting ready for school, they often tell their mother, 'Baba is the chief guest at an event being organized in school.' Or sometimes they come home waving the questionnaire of a quiz contest that has questions about Eco-Pro and Bandu Dhotre. Their faces beam with pride as they tell their mother, 'Our friends in school look at us in disbelief and are awestruck when we tell them that we are Bandu Dhotre's sons.'

But Chitraksh and Rudraksh have never enjoyed the simple pleasures of family life, like having ice cream in the summer or going on a picnic in winter. 'Your father does not have the time and I don't have the money for such outings,' their mother explains to them. This leads to angry outbursts. 'I don't ever want to be like him,' the older of the two brothers shouts as his mother looks on helplessly, not finding the right words that can both pacify her son and not damage the respect she knows he has for his father. She confronts Bandu when he comes home. 'I have no answer when they ask me why their father, who is such a celebrated figure, cannot provide for their requirements,' Yojana tells her husband. 'Scrounging up even Rs 100 for their needs is a struggle as I never have any money to spare.'

Bandu admits that he has not been an ideal father. 'Once I bought the wrong set of textbooks for them. I didn't even know which class they were in,' he rues. They had admitted their sons to a neighbourhood school, but the monthly fee of Rs 250 was more than what the family could afford. The boys would have been denied an education if a friend of Bandu's had not come to know of their predicament. He arranged for a sponsor to fund the boys' education. Both of Bandu's sons now study in a public school and their fees are taken care of by benevolent patrons.

This does not bother Bandu. 'The only way to success is through talent, hard work, and a grasp on life and what to make of it,' he says. 'It depends upon the boys—what they make of their lives. If they have the talent and capability, the roads to success will open up for them.'

Yojana's suffering, however, is something that does hurt Bandu. It makes him feel inadequate and helpless. She, on her part, is constantly torn between pride in her husband's work and the struggles she goes through for money and his attention. She is proud of the name and fame that her husband has earned, but frustrated that he doesn't earn enough to sustain their family.

The hurt surfaces as rancour in petty, daily matters. Riding on his bike, she insists that he take a particular route to reach their destination. 'We will get caught in a traffic jam, as I know that there is a procession coming down that road,' he explains to her. Adamant that she have her way, she insists that he take the route she wants. He does, and both spend more than half an hour stuck in a jam. 'I can sense what's going to happen next. Yojana can't. She lives in the present and that's why she suffers,' is how Bandu sums up their constant friction.

The lofty goals he has set for himself trouble his wife. She constantly tries to strike a balance between giving him the freedom to attain them and her longing to remain relevant in his life. 'He feels he is born to do great things in life. Being his wife, I can't come in the way of his achieving them. But as his wife I also have some expectations from him,' she says.

She also questions whether working so much for society actually does any good; she questions the cost the family has to pay for it. She finds his selfless acts utterly selfish, performed for personal gratification. However, despite all the contradictions that life has heaped upon her, Yojana would not like to change anything. 'He is a good man,' she repeats, as if to reassure herself. 'I want my sons to be like their father and work with Eco-Pro.'

Bandu, however, doesn't want anybody—neither his sons nor any of his volunteers—to become another Bandu Dhotre. He knows that keeping personal ambition at bay while riding success and fame needs a great deal of moral and mental strength. 'I am completely involved in my work and have no time for anything else. It is a tough act to follow,' he warns. He admits that at heart and in his mind he is no better than a sadhu, albeit one with a family.

Bandu has remained incorruptible. For him, Chandrapur comes first—that is what fuels him. The campaigns of Eco-Pro have been run without budgets as the organization has no money. It is a difficult path that he has chosen—he was even caught on camera being attacked by a leopard that had strayed into a town while he was trying to rescue it—though recognition has repeatedly come his way.

In 2019, Eco-Pro received the National Youth Award from India's youth welfare and sports ministry. The credibility he enjoys in Chandrapur gets him the inevitable attention from political parties. He steadfastly ignores them—he thinks politics can ruin the reputation that he has so painstakingly built over the years.

The Good Samaritan of Chandrapur does not believe in God, but believes there is a power that propels him. It takes the form of an inner voice or a vision that helps him see how things will shape up, he says. Bandu's circumstances prevented him from being an army man, but he was able to harness all his dejections into a meaningful and powerful force. He is a soldier at heart, waging wars for the greater good of his people.

Sitting on a chair in one of the two tiny rooms in his house, Bandu looks out beyond the door. His pain at the misery of his family reflects in his eyes and casts a shadow on his face. But the irrepressible spirit in him bounces back. He has work to do. He plans to build a new house, hopefully with a bit more space for the ten people who now make up the joint family, although two of his brothers and his sister have moved out after their weddings. And Bandu Dhotre still has causes to fight for.

'I will never give up,' he says. 'I have hope that if I keep faith in this power, I will surely succeed.'

Ravindra and Smita Kolhe

SELFLESS SERVICE AS THEIR LIFELONG MOTTO

Man's ultimate aim is the realization of God … The only way to find God is to see Him in His creation and be one with it. This can only be done by service of all. I am a part and parcel of the whole, and I cannot find Him apart from the rest of humanity. My countrymen are my nearest neighbours. They have become so helpless, so resourceless, so inert that I must concentrate myself on serving them. If I could persuade myself that I should find Him in a Himalayan cave I would proceed there immediately. But I know that I cannot find Him apart from humanity.

— Mohandas Karamchand Gandhi, writing in the *Harijan* on 29 August 1936.[1]

1 Nirmal Kumar Bose, *Selections from Gandhi* (Ahmedabad: Navajivan Publishing House, 1936), www.mkgandhi.org https://archive.org/details/HindSwaraj.Harijan.vol4

An eerie silence had descended at dusk over the tiny hamlet of Bairagarh, tucked away between green hillocks on the banks of the Sipna river in the Melghat region of Amravati. A silence broken only by the shouts and abuses from an SUV full of leering, burly men. Across from them, in a chair outside a mud house, sat a diminutive man, his grey beard covering most of his face. A rickety bamboo gate was all that stood between him and the men, who were clearly there to beat him up—or maybe worse—and looking for the slightest excuse to do so.

The man's wife, who was cooking over a firewood stove, was growing more worried and agitated with every passing minute. 'Let them be,' the man said to calm her down. 'After all, they are only giving me something, even if it is filthy abuse, and not taking anything from me.' The men continued to draw closer, their words and actions growing more violent and menacing. The man nonchalantly sat through it all. He simply refused to react.

Dr Ravindra Kolhe, who has, for the past thirty-five years, lived in Bairagarh with his wife, homeopathy practitioner Smita Kolhe, does not hold the incident, which happened in 1992, against the villagers. That night, the hired goons left—without even eating the dinner prepared for them by the ones who had hired them—when they could not provoke Ravindra.

'I knew that if I didn't react they would get suspicious, thinking maybe I had a plan up my sleeve,' he says, chuckling. 'And when you are trying to bring about social change, such friction happens.'

The evil and the wicked are often big cowards, Ravindra says; it's wisdom he has gleaned from the teachings of Mahatma Gandhi and Vinoba Bhave.

Dr Ravindra and Dr Smita Kolhe have lived Bapu's philosophy—of service to God through service to mankind. Ravindra chose

Bairagarh, where wild animals roamed and hunger stalked, because he felt that his service was needed the most there. Smita also gave up the life she had known, and chose to be his true partner in service and healing to a people who were being killed by preventable diseases.

On a good day, Ravindra, usually dressed in a khadi shirt and pyjamas, can be seen whizzing across the village on his white scooter. His soft-spoken nature, keen eyes and wrinkled forehead all combine to give him a slightly lost, vulnerable look. But frail is not an adjective that can be used for the man who has single-handedly brought healthcare to this part of the tribal heartland of Maharashtra and chased away the shadow of malnutrition hanging over it.

Ravindra and Smita settled down in Bairagarh in 1988. By then, Ravindra had already been there for four years. The people in the hundred-odd households—mostly Muslim and tribal—survived off the land and lived in abject poverty, like they had for centuries. There was no electricity, no medical facility—not even a ration shop to dispense foodgrains. Ravindra had chosen the area with meticulous planning, to be able to serve those most in need. The couple had to undergo innumerable trials by fire before the people of Bairagarh accepted them as healers. Like that night with the goons.

~

The seeds of service to the impoverished and neglected rural population had been sown early in Ravindra Kolhe's mind—by his life experiences, the people he came in touch with and the books he read. Good books can change your life, he is fond of saying. It is something he has learnt over the course of his life.

Ravindra was diagnosed with a heart ailment, pulmonary hypertension, soon after he was born in the temple town of Shegaon in Buldhana district of Maharashtra. His father worked in the railways and his mother was a schoolteacher. Ravindra grew up with many restrictions imposed on him due to his poor health. He was constantly in and out of hospitals—something the family could not have afforded had medical aid and travel not been free for railway employees.

Physical exercise and exertion were ruled out for him. He was so fragile that, at times, he needed support or had to be carried to his class. To fight the loneliness and lack of activity, Ravindra surrounded himself with books and buried himself deep in them, reading voraciously. His mother quit her job to take care of him. She also took refuge in spirituality, visiting the town's famous temple of Gajanan Maharaj, where she would read the scriptures and discuss them with priests and holy men. Ravindra began to accompany his mother on these trips. He began to imbibe the teachings from the sermons given by saints who visited the temple, and the discussions his mother would have with them. When his mother could not visit the temple, he filled in for her and read out from the scriptures to the people gathered there.

In school, he could not take part in most sports events and cultural activities. However, his knowledge of varied subjects and the teachings of great men made him a much-sought-after speaker on occasions such as Gandhi Jayanti and Independence Day. After the Class X board exams, he had to shift out of Shegaon; the paucity of money and his frail health made Wardha, where his maternal aunt lived, the best option. Ravindra's uncle was a staunch Gandhian, and the young boy's exposure to the life, journeys and thoughts of great men continued under the tutelage of his uncle. Ravindra would spend time with him, learning about Gandhian thought and the philosophy espoused by Vinoba Bhave, whose ashram at Pavnar was near Wardha. Whatever free time Ravindra had was spent in a library close to their house.

A high score in the Class XII board exams gave Ravindra a choice between a career in engineering and one in medicine. His uncle advised him to opt for medicine, as 'an engineer works with machines, but a doctor works on people'. The urge to serve the needy and the poor had already begun to take root in Ravindra's mind, thanks to the teachings of Gandhi, which had left a deep impression on him. Sure of the path he wanted to pursue, Ravindra took admission in the Government Medical College in Nagpur in 1980.

Good books, thoughts of great men and knowledgeable people were what he always looked for. He found all of these at the Ramakrishna Mission. He began visiting the *math* regularly to read in its library and interact with its monks. Their austere life and deep philosophy impressed young Ravindra, who began to seriously consider giving up the worldly life to become an ascetic. The learned monks patiently explained to him that even the greatest of sages had led a family life before they renounced the world.

At medical college too, besides studies, Ravindra searched for a higher purpose in life. He found a few kindred, idealistic students. Soon, a group of budding doctors started meeting after classes to hold esoteric discussions and explore ways to lead a meaningful life. Service to mankind became the focal theme. By the time they were in their final year, the group had a name, Sangharsh, meaning struggle. The members of Sangharsh started providing medical aid to the residents of a slum behind their college. As their MBBS course approached its end, the members of Sangharsh began to struggle with their plans for the future. It was crucial for all of them to get jobs or set up a medical practice. Another option was to appear for the civil services exam. Ravindra discussed it with his professor. His teacher and mentor, Professor Jaju, dissuaded him. 'You will clear the exam and become a collector. Then you will give orders, but their implementation will not be entirely in your hands. But as a doctor, you will have the capability to treat patients, cure them and provide relief. The results would be lifelong,' the professor advised. Ravindra readily accepted it.

The young doctors found themselves at a crossroads again when it came to the choice of internship after their completion of MBBS. Ravindra and his batchmates checked out the possibilities at thirty-seven places. A huge inspiration for many young doctors was the work done by Dr Prakash and Dr Mandakani Amte at Hemalkasa in Gadchiroli, which members of Sangharsh had been visiting. However, Ravindra opted to spend a month of his internship at Tapovan, run by Dr Shivajirao Patwardhan in Amravati.

On the advice of Mahatma Gandhi, Dr Patwardhan had formed the Vidarbha Maharogi Seva Mandal for the relief and rehabilitation of leprosy patients. The Mahatma had suggested that he start rehabilitation work along with treatment, and also infuse self-confidence in those afflicted with leprosy. The facility at Amravati was inaugurated by Vinoba Bhave in 1950 and later came to be known as Tapovan.

The methods and approach of Dr Patwardhan impressed Ravindra. The senior doctor was in his nineties when Ravindra arrived at Tapovan for his internship. He would meet Dr Patwardhan every day. The doctor would give him a book to read. Once Ravindra had finished reading, the two would discuss it. The exercise helped Ravindra firm up his thoughts on service to mankind, especially through the book *Unto This Last* by John Ruskin, which left a lasting impression on Ravindra. Gandhi is also said to have been influenced by this book, which he discovered during his stay in South Africa.

Ravindra happened to come across another book, *Where There Is No Doctor* by David Werner. The cover was a picture of four men carrying a patient near a milestone that read: 'Hospital: 30 miles.' It showed Ravindra the direction he had to take. Being a follower of Gandhian principles, he had already decided to spend his life serving people in a rural area. Now he knew where he had to go—a place from where the closest hospital was 30 miles away. He began to explore areas in Karnataka, Gujarat and Madhya Pradesh that bordered Maharashtra—areas where medical facilities tend to thin and disappear. In the villages on the border of Maharashtra and Madhya Pradesh, Ravindra heard about a place called Bairagarh, where several children died of diarrhoea every day, pneumonia cases were rampant, no treatment was available for tuberculosis and childbirth mortality was high. At that time in the 1980s, all transport towards Bairagarh ended at Harisal, from where one had to walk 40 kilometres.

The decision was daunting, his seniors pointed out. 'To work in such a remote area, you will need to know three things: to deliver a baby single-handedly without any facility, diagnose pneumonia without an X-ray and be able to treat diarrhoea,' his professors told him. Ravindra took up an intensive course in mother and child care at Bombay Hospital in Maharashtra's capital city to acquire these skills, before leaving for Bairagarh. Equipped with all the knowledge that he could garner, he reached Bairagarh on 9 February 1985, along with his friend and batchmate Dr Dilip Ghandkeri.

There was no concrete structure in sight and no place they could rent, so the doctors set up their clinic under a tree. Both of them had decided that they would stay for a month and if they did not get patients, would return and take up government jobs. They received three patients on their very first day.

Besides the training, one piece of advice from their professors that the young doctors carried with them was that they should not provide free service. The two doctors decided to charge Re 1 from each patient and provide medicines at cost prices. However, the people in the village were so poor that the medicines had to be provided for free. Being a follower of the Maharashtrian saint Gadge Maharaj, who begged from others, for others, all his life, Ravindra decided that if he fell short of money, he would also beg to provide treatment to the poor. When a snakebite victim arrived with no money for treatment, the two doctors begged around in the village and managed to collect Rs 109. The treatment cost was Rs 120. They had to pitch in with the balance amount of Rs 11.

Six months after Ravindra came to Bairagarh, his father arrived to see how his son was doing. When he reached the village and asked for his son, he was led to the tree under which Ravindra had set up his clinic. His father sat at a distance, watching his son attend to patients. This was definitely not how he had visualized his son practising medicine. When the last of the patients had been examined, Ravindra and his father walked to the courtyard of a mud house. A tribal man had magnanimously allowed Ravindra to sleep outside his house. Ravindra's luggage and the few belongings he had were placed neatly along one wall. A mat that served as his bed at night stood folded in one corner. His father could take no more—he was distraught at the thought of his son, who suffered from a congenital heart disease, sleeping on the cold and damp floor. 'There is no need for you to suffer such hardship. You can live in your home and still serve the poor,' he tried to reason with Ravindra. For the idealistic doctor, however, there was no going back. After staying in Bairagarh for barely a day, his father returned to Shegaon with a heavy heart.

When Ravindra went to Shegaon to celebrate Diwali with his family, an uncle asked him about his plans. 'I have identified a village in Melghat and will be living there to serve the poor people,' Ravindra told him. When his father heard of this, he was aghast. 'Will you not take up a job?' he asked his son. The festival of lights turned into one of gloom for the family. Ravindra's parents were stricken with worry over how their frail son would survive such physical hardship in such a remote area.

A long argument ensued between him and his parents. But Ravindra was unflinching in his resolve. 'The upbringing you have given me has taught me to feel for the poor and serve the needy,' he told his parents. Recalling the many occasions when he had to be rushed to the hospital during his childhood, he also told them, 'I could survive this ailment only because of the constant and prompt medical care I got. I want to make sure that the needy in villages also get this opportunity.'

In the end, his parents gave up, bitter. 'You will never ask us or expect any financial help from us,' they told Ravindra.

In Bairagarh, the two doctors continued to battle illnesses, death and misery. The sheer number of mothers and infants who succumbed to various diseases in front of their eyes shattered them. They realized that they were ill equipped to wage this war, that an MBBS doctor could do little in such a remote area, where even aspirin was not available. If they wanted to bring about any substantial change, they would have to know more. Both the doctors decided to return and do their postgraduate studies. Many in the village wagered that they would not come back.

Though his friend Dilip left Bairagarh after four months of their arrival there, Ravindra could not get admission to the postgraduate course immediately. So he stayed back for one-and-a-half years until he got admission. He carried back from Bairagarh some crucial lessons he had learnt, such as the importance of early diagnosis and prompt treatment—which could happen only when doctors were within reach. Ravindra decided to come back after getting his postgraduate degree in preventive and social medicine. He, however, knew that his friend wouldn't be accompanying him back to Bairagarh as he was getting married and his wife was not keen to live in a remote village.

As Ravindra completed his post-graduation, he began to realize that he could not return to Bairagarh without a partner—he would not be able to serve the people there all alone. He decided that he had to get married, but to a girl who shared his sense of purpose. He also realized that he had to get married while he was in Nagpur. Once he returned to Bairagarh, it would be impossible to find someone to come and live there.

He reached out to his friends and well-wishers, and set four qualities that the bride needed to have. She should be willing to walk 40 kilometres, be ready to manage the house in Rs 400 (the number of patients he would see in a month for a fee of Re 1), agree to a court marriage shorn of pomp on an expenditure of Rs 5, and be ready to beg for others if need be.

It was, however, not the kind of life any girl was likely to want to have.

Smita remembers the day she became 'Doctor Kolhe' from 'Nursebai' to the people of Bairagarh. It was the day she put 450 stitches on a man who had been mauled by a tiger. The man was critical and Ravindra was away. 'Don't touch this patient as this is a forest case—there will be an inquiry,' she was told when the man, bleeding profusely, had been brought in. She knew she had to help him, or it would be too late. She rushed inside the house where she lived with Ravindra, and to the altar—praying and gathering the inner strength required—before deciding to stitch up the man.

Smita often hums old Bollywood songs as she prepares a simple meal in the kitchen, clad in a khadi sari and a khadi blouse. Her love for music is all that has remained with her from her life before marriage. Watching her go about her task in her modest and sparsely furnished home in Bairagarh makes it difficult to visualize her as the fashionably dressed woman she used to be three decades ago. The kind who would drive all across town to find the right pair of footwear to match her sari.

Smita Manjare was the youngest of ten siblings, of whom only six survived. Her father, like Ravindra's, was a railway employee, though he hailed from a family of jewellers. Her mother was indifferent to her, Smita says, perhaps because she had hoped to give birth to another boy. Smita says she grew up feeling unwanted and neglected. The passing away of her mother, when Smita was in her early teens, made matters worse. She was the youngest, and there was a big age gap between Smita and her five brothers. As they all got married and settled down, she felt she was seen as an additional responsibility that nobody wanted to bear.

The family, which lived in the Mahal area of Nagpur, where the Rashtriya Swayamsevak Sangh (RSS) has its headquarters, believed in the ideology of the RSS. The sangh had a huge influence on Smita. During the Emergency in 1975, Smita and others in the family had clandestinely carried documents and pamphlets for Opposition leaders in hiding. One of her friends was Nitin Gadkari, who is now a senior Bharatiya Janata Party (BJP) leader and Union minister. Like Gadkari, Smita was a member of the Akhil Bharatiya Vidyarthi Parishad (ABVP), the student wing of the RSS. At that time, Gadkari was studying law and Smita, too, wanted to join the course. However, she was wary of telling her father. She was not sure he would be able to afford the course fee.

Smita joined a fine arts course, but her restless spirit constantly pushed her to do new things, such as join the National Cadet Corps (NCC) as an under officer. She says her commanding officer, Kamal Dafftrey, made a huge impact on her. Being part of the first batch of the NCC air wing in Nagpur, Smita enjoyed gliding and parachuting, which gave flight to her free spirit. She also acquired a bachelor's degree in music after finishing the course on fine arts, but it was important for her to be financially independent. She knew that it would be difficult to make a career out of music. Postgraduate studies seemed impossible as her father had retired by then. When she was twenty, Smita developed a skin ailment, due to which white spots began to appear on her body. The attitude of her family towards her turned even more hostile. They were convinced that nobody would marry her and that she would be a permanent liability to them.

Used to apathy and indifference from her family, Smita tried to get the spots treated herself. She visited an elderly and well-known doctor of the city. Far from treating her problem, the doctor preyed on her. He would insist that he check her alone in his chamber. Whoever was accompanying her had to stay outside. Inside, he groped her. Shattered, traumatized and angry, Smita stopped the treatment after a while. She could not share the humiliation with anybody—she knew no one would help her. The trauma that sexual abuse survivors go through is well documented, and Smita, too, was drawn into a vortex of depression. She stayed at home for two months. With no one to share her fears and apprehensions with, she battled her demons alone. In the end, it was her grit and fighting spirit that helped her bounce back.

She had wanted to study law, but her lack of proficiency in English was a major obstacle. Now she decided that she had to give it a shot. She enrolled herself on an LLB course and convinced her father to pay her fees. In the late 1970s, very few Indian women took up law. Many among her family and friends ridiculed her, often joking about how a woman would behave in a courtroom. It was an era when sexist remarks were part of everyday humour. Not one to be cowed down, Smita struggled on. However, English was not her strong point and she could barely follow what was being taught in class. She would take down copious notes, and once home, would try to understand the words with the help of an English-to-Hindi dictionary. However, in the second year of law, when Smita began to attend court, she realized that this was not what she wanted to do. A family friend noticed Smita's confusion. He introduced her to a course in homoeopathy at a college close to her home. For four years, she divided her day between attending law classes in the morning and homoeopathy lectures in the evening. She went on to clear both courses.

Oblivious to the efforts that Smita was putting in, her family's focus was only on getting her married somehow. They began to scout for a match for her. It was also decided that her skin problem would not be disclosed to the suitors. For the righteous Smita, this was unacceptable.

Tired of the hostile environment at home, she approached her father and asked for money to set up a homoeopathy clinic. 'You are ready to give gold at my wedding, so why don't you invest that money and help me stand on my feet?' she reasoned with him. She knew her father would agree, and he did. Smita honed her skills in administering medicines by working with Vilas Dangre, a noted homoeopathy practitioner in west Nagpur. After training her for nearly four years, he told Smita that she was ready to set up an independent practice. Eager to do so, she began to look for a place.

In 1984, the year Ravindra graduated from medical college, Smita was busy setting up her clinic. Shriram Joshi, an RSS member, offered her a shop he owned in Mahal, close to where she lived. When she asked him about the rent, he quipped, 'What rent? Your practice will not run, so how will you pay for it?' Undeterred by such negative remarks, Smita took up the offer. It was a ramshackle shop, but she transformed it aesthetically, including using a flower vase that a brother had got on his wedding. Smita would put flowers in it every day. One day a handcart loaded with a table and a few chairs landed at her clinic. They were a gift from her friend Nitin Gadkari, who had set up a furniture business and knew of her requirements at the new clinic. With the clinic in place, Smita was in business. On the very first day there were fifteen patients. Her niece, who had come with her to the clinic, dispensed medicines in tiny white packets.

Smita charged Rs 5 for eight visits, and had a steady stream of patients. Life began to look up for her. She was always an aesthete, and Smita now began to indulge herself by buying trendy saris, accessories and jewellery. As her earnings and influence grew, she became the family's favourite. But there was change and churning within Smita. There were questions within her that the best of saris and jewellery did not hold answers to. Larger questions about life. She had started reading the Bhagavad Gita. Its narrative of renunciation and sacrifice began to change her outlook towards life.

Even as she began to search for true meaning and purpose, her successful homoeopathy practice started getting noticed by her community. To the delight of her family, matrimonial proposals began arriving by the dozens. Her brothers and sisters-in-law began to entertain them. Families of suitable boys were invited to the Manjare home to meet the prospective bride. Hordes of relatives arrived, along with the boy. Acting demure, Smita would carry a tray loaded with poha and tea for the guests. She could feel their eyes on her. After a couple of visits, Smita told her family, 'From now on I will meet these boys at my clinic.' It had a seismic impact on the Manjare household, but Smita stood her ground. Many young men did visit her clinic. 'I will close down the clinic after marriage and you will have to provide for me,' she would tell them. They would scoot.

Smita was certain about getting married, but on her own terms. It was also the only way out of the stifling environment at home, where everyone seemed eager to get rid of her. Smita started asking around for matches for herself. Dressed elegantly in fashionable saris and accessories, she began visiting select addresses in her quest for a life partner. Her visits proved to be a source of acute embarrassment for the eligible young men. It unnerved them, this turning of the tables on what was a tradition in middle-class Indian households. Though they did not carry a tray laden with tea and snacks, the boys would become self-conscious. Acutely aware of her gaze on them, they would clumsily adjust their shirt collars and fidget around while facing a barrage of questions from her.

Smita's unconventional methods of looking for a groom did not meet with success, until a friend who knew Ravindra suggested that she meet him. The friend also told Smita about the conditions the doctor had laid down for his future wife. This piqued her curiosity. However, it took her two months to make up her mind. She finally asked the friend to arrange a meeting.

Ravindra arrived at Smita's clinic on a summer evening in 1988, wearing his usual simple khadi kurta-pyjama. It was a busy day and a large number of patients were waiting to consult her. When he entered the clinic, he saw a number of young girls there and began to wonder which one was Smita. Two of Smita's nieces were also present at the clinic. Ravindra occupied the corner of a bench and began to take in the scene at the busy clinic, unaware that Smita was observing him from behind the tinted glass that separated her cabin and the waiting area.

After more than an hour and a half, when the last of the patients had left, Ravindra was called in. One look at the stylishly dressed woman wearing lipstick and jewellery, and he was done. This was not how he had imagined her to be. There was no way she would agree to live in a village. He was ready to leave when she stopped him and offered him a glass of water. He accepted and took a seat. She began to make small talk, starting with the weather. Gradually, the two began to warm up to each other. Matters of mutual interest, their work and their lives were brought up. The discussion veered to service, renunciation and austerity. The meeting stretched for over three hours and ended with the two deciding to tie the knot. Not one to take any chances, Ravindra asked her to close her practice and shut down the clinic first. Only then would he give a month's notice in court for the marriage. His fear was that if they married first, she would continue practising at the clinic. He was not aware that this was what Smita had wanted. She readily agreed. They got married in a court in Nagpur on 8 December 1988.

Smita Kolhe is as unlike Smita Manjare as could be. From the time she got married, she has only worn saris worth Rs 10 available at ration shops. When Ravindra and Smita moved to Bairagarh as husband and wife, their house made of bamboo and mud was built with the help of villagers who contributed by way of labour and material. It had two rooms. The kitchen occupied one portion, where a mud *chulha* (stove) was set up. The only piece of furniture was a dresser with a full-size mirror. Smita would go with the village women to collect firewood. Her mornings were spent preparing a mixture of cow dung, fodder and water with which she would slather the floor and walls of her new home. She found beauty—and inner peace—in the grace of performing chores such as cleaning the glass chimney and placing it over the kerosene lamp and balancing herself on the ledge of the village well to draw water. In the clean and invigorating environment of Bairagarh, her skin spots also disappeared.

The couple did have their share of quarrels, though. Cooking became a bone of contention. Being the youngest in her family, and with her sisters-in-law taking charge of the kitchen, Smita had never felt the need to cook. Ravindra had assured her that he could cook, but she soon discovered that he knew nothing about it. The arguments would mostly be about how to cook, followed by recriminations. 'You can't even distinguish between salt and sugar—how would you know what goes into preparing a dish?' she would say. 'I can prepare a meal for myself—you will have to develop a taste for it', was the answer she would get. Finally, with some help and largely by trial and error, Smita took the easier way out by learning to put together a simple meal.

She missed having conversations. Smita is articulate and enjoys talking. Her husband is a man of few words, who enjoys solitude and enriching himself through self-analysis and silent introspection. The natural beauty of Melghat acted as a balm for all the little hurts Smita had to accept. The lashing rains in the monsoons turn the area lush green and misty. The harsh summers bake it brown. The winters add a nip to the air and spring brings the fragrances of flowers in bloom. Smita would walk down to the banks of the Sipna and sit there, gazing at the muddy froth when the river was in spate. 'I would link the roar of the water to the anger and pent-up emotions raging in my heart and mind, desperately looking for an outlet. But sitting there, I could feel the river washing away the commotion in my mind,' she reminisces.

Nitin Gadkari, whom she considers a brother, visited her in Bairagarh in 1995, when he was the Public Works Department minister in the Maharashtra government. Incidentally, it was Rakshabandhan that day. He was appalled to see her living in a mud house, and promised to get a proper one built for her. Turning down the offer, she asked him to build a road from Dharni block of Melghat to Bairagarh, as it would benefit the entire area.

In the open space near their mud house, Ravindra had built two rooms that served as the clinic and hospital. A tuberculosis ward was also set up. As Smita watched while her husband examined patients, she began to realize that the villagers did not consider her a doctor. She was just a 'nursebai' assisting the doctor. Soon, this began to irk her. She asked her husband, who was training many young doctors coming to him for internships, to teach her allopathic medicine as she had to assist him. But Ravindra did not do so.

'I was not training random people,' he explains. 'Those coming to me, such as Dr Ashish Satav, were already qualified medical professionals. I was training them on how to treat the diseases that were more prevalent in this tribal region.'

But life, as usual, had other plans. Smita had been performing deliveries, and quite complicated ones at that. One day, a call came from a village near the Madhya Pradesh border. The woman had been in labour for three days. Smita, who was running a high fever, decided she had to go. With no means of transport available, she hitched a ride on a bullock cart to reach the village. There, she found the woman in a deplorable state. It was a case of a prolapsed hand of the infant. The baby was dead, but the desire to live burnt in the eyes of the unfortunate, ailing mother. With the entire village standing and watching from outside, Smita began treatment inside the hut with the little equipment she had carried with her. She had a defective saline pouch, which had no place to punch a hole. She asked around for a long needle used for stitching. Once it was provided, she heated it on a flame to sterilize it and then pierced the pouch with it. As the liquid began to flow, she got down to work. After a lot of effort, the woman delivered the dead baby. It was an extremely emotional moment, and both patient and doctor wept in relief as well as sorrow. Seeing the woman's fragile condition, Smita brought her to Bairagarh and nursed her back to health. Smita sent her off in the traditional way, by buying her new bangles and gifting her a sari.

Then came the tiger-attack victim. After that, the villagers began to address Smita as 'Doctor'.

~

The philosophy that Dr Ravindra and Smita Kolhe live by helps them find new meaning to life even in the toughest situations. Smita sincerely believes that if a person has a pure heart,

God protects them and keeps failures away. 'The woman I had treated became pregnant again two years later, but died during delivery. I could save her the first time because my intentions were pure. We are not here to make money, but to serve people. So people also place a lot of trust in us. We are able to treat them because of our strength in our convictions,' she says.

Ravindra and Smita's sons, Rohit and Ram, were both born in Bairagarh. Like new life always does, the birth of their sons sealed the couple's relationship with the villagers, while also testing their determination to stay in the village and serve them.

When Smita got pregnant the first time, Ravindra had decided that she would deliver her baby in Bairagarh, like other village women. Certain complications during the delivery, however, led to their son developing meningitis, pneumonia and septicaemia. Alarmed at the condition of the newborn, well-wishers suggested that both mother and child be moved to a hospital in Akola, a city about 178 kilometres away. Ravindra was torn between concern for his newborn child and the commitment to the village. Finally, he left the decision to Smita.

'I would prefer to stay here and have you treat the child,' she told her husband, realizing how crucial this decision was to him. Smita's faith bore fruit once again. Rohit recovered and both parents heaved a sigh of relief. 'Had I left Bairagarh at that moment, I would never have been able to show my face to these villagers,' says Ravindra.

Ravindra had arrived in Bairagarh to improve the healthcare situation in the village and bring down mortality rates. In his mission, he was helped by the knowledge of his seniors. His professors had told him that duplication of work would not serve any purpose. For example, they said, it was the job of the government to ensure vaccination in the village. His job was to put pressure on the government agencies to perform—by collaborating and, wherever required, through questioning.

In the year 2000, nearly fifteen years after Ravindra had arrived in Bairagarh, a government primary healthcare centre opened there. This considerably reduced the load of medical cases on the doctor. When the dial-108 ambulance facility started, he began referring cases to the primary healthcare centre. It took some time to strike up a rapport with the healthcare workers there, who viewed the couple as unwanted pressure on them to do their duties. The staff at the centre would refuse to treat patients who came in after 5 p.m. The doctor there once refused to see the sarpanch—the village head—and asked him to come back the next day as the outpatient hours were over. The livid sarpanch returned to the medical centre with a gun, forcing the doctor to see him. The doctor lodged a police complaint. The situation was brought under control by Ravindra, as the district healthcare officer had been his batchmate. The healthcare centre's doctor was persuaded to take back the complaint.

Dr Ravindra and Smita Kolhe's push for bringing about change in partnership with the government machinery gained momentum when Praveen Pardeshi, the then CEO of Zilla Parishad Amravati district, visited Bairagarh in 1991. Seeing that the officer was willing to walk the extra mile, Ravindra told him in detail about the various issues plaguing the area. He managed to draw the attention of the administration towards the glaring problems of the region and also secure employment for the local youth.

The scope of the Kolhes' work began to widen when the healthcare situation in the village improved considerably. Believing that the doctor had a cure for every problem, the villagers would approach him with their crop-related issues as well. They would bring the dying stems of tur plants with a fungal infection and ask him to do something about it. Ravindra took it upon himself to find a solution for their agriculture-related problems as well. He visited the Dr Panjabrao Deshmukh Krishi Vidyapeeth in Nagpur, where he consulted research scientists and learnt of measures that the people of Bairagarh could adopt to increase their income.

~

The couple's presence in the village has been healing and holistic—even beyond providing medical help and agricultural guidance. When the couple first settled down in the village, Smita would hear about the rampant sexual exploitation of tribal women, which perturbed her immensely. She began to fight for their rights and gave these women, long used to subjugation, a voice of their own.

Some of these battles crossed over into their personal lives. When she raised her voice against the sexual exploitation of village women, people would come to their house and abuse them. 'They would block the door of my house, shouting and threatening to beat us up,' says Smita. 'Ravi could not physically fight with them because of his health. But I have the strength to hold them by the collar and throw them out.'

In 1992, when a local tribal man complained to them about his fourteen-year-old son being converted to Islam, the couple were in a quandary. Ravindra insisted that this did not merit their intervention as they were doctors, but Smita felt otherwise. 'We had a discussion the entire night, where I argued that the law said it was illegal to convert a minor. It was wrong and we had to oppose it.' But Ravindra felt that such things were beyond their purview. 'Our work should not go beyond providing medical care,' he reasoned with his wife. Tired of arguing, Smita told him, 'I will go even if you don't come.' Finally, the doctor decided to stand by his wife. The boy's father had complained that his son had been taken to the mosque and allegedly fed beef. The tribal community would now not take him back. But Ravindra knew the food served at the mosque was mostly rice and dal, which the boy may have eaten because he was famished.

This incident brought the situation in the village to a flashpoint between tribals and Muslims. About 3,000 tribals from across Melghat gathered to beat up the Muslims in the village. 'I told them that they would have to beat me up first,' Ravindra says, remembering the incident. 'I reasoned with them, saying that the tribals living here would have to bear the brunt of their actions. Who would protect them later?' The doctor asked the mob to find out why the boy had gone to the mosque. 'He went out of sheer hunger, I explained to them,' Ravindra says. He had turned a communally charged situation into one in which the spotlight was focused on more pressing problems such as hunger and unemployment. Most of them blamed lack of employment for their miserable state. 'I told them then that we needed to create more employment for the youth here,' Ravindra says.

The episode did put the Kolhes in a perilous situation. It was over this that the goons had arrived at their doorstep. There were also attempts to destroy his medical practice. The locals would spread rumours that patients who went there for treatment died. A bogus doctor was also brought in to complain against them. Ravindra, in turn, sent a bogus patient to the bogus doctor and filed a police complaint about it. The imposter had to go back. Revealing the warrior hidden under the guise of a monk, Ravindra dismisses any talk of his being a gentleman. 'I am not. Both Gandhi and Vinoba Bhave say that if you have to fight injustice, you will have to answer it the same way, otherwise you will not be able to brave it. You will be termed a coward.'

The respect the villagers have for Dr Ravindra and Smita Kolhe has only grown because the couple always practise what they preach. Their sons were admitted to the village school, though many suggested they attend an English-medium school in a nearby city.

'Rohit and Ram would often come home from school and complain about some of their teachers smoking bidi in the classroom,' says Ravindra, who feels that by sending their sons to the local school, they could learn much about what was happening in the village. The father then asked his sons to sort out the issue themselves by telling the teacher that smoking was injurious to health. 'Their presence in the school also proved beneficial as it helped in weeding out many such problems,' Ravindra adds.

~

It took the Kolhes three decades of relentless work to effect change in the face of stiff opposition. 'In the end, I have been able to reform those very people who had once tried to push liquor down my young son's throat,' Smita recalls. Today, Ravindra and Smita know most locals by name. Everyone, of course, knows them.

The decades of hardship have taken a toll on Smita's health. Living in a mud house for three decades in the wet and humid climate of Melghat has resulted in severe arthritis leading to knee-replacement surgeries. They now live in a concrete house built by their elder son, where their makeshift hospital once stood. The mud house still stands, a reminder of their early days in Bairagarh.

The apparent contrast in the personalities of Ravindra and Smita has worked for both of them. She is a firebrand and he has a sobering effect on her in volatile situations. 'Ravi did suffer on my account—he has told me so. Ravindra is frail because of his health condition. But I am aggressive and can take on people and situations. This has sometimes got us into trouble,' Smita says. 'He is an honest man. His commitment to his work is absolute, and he takes it to its logical conclusion. He never hurts anyone. And that's what I like the most about him.'

Dr Ravindra and Smita Kolhe were awarded the Padma Shri, India's fourth-highest civilian honour, in 2019 for their work and service to the people of Bairagarh. The two of them, however, do not see themselves as extraordinary. They are dismissive of any attribution of charity to their work. 'We came here to live the way we wanted to. Service was the by-product. Through the Gita we tried to understand the purpose of life. Ours was a journey of self-discovery, and we enjoy doing this,' says Ravindra, summing up their belief. 'They did not ask us to come here and serve or treat them,' Smita adds. 'It was our desire to do so.'

Mohan and Devaji

SARVODAYA IN THE JUNGLES OF CENTRAL INDIA

A truck ride changed the life of Mohan Hirabai Hiralal. It gave him, an affluent businessman's son with a penchant for reading, a glimpse of the world he wanted to explore—the jungles of central India, where the tribals, the original inhabitants of the land, live. It would be deep in those forests of Gadchiroli, in the village of Mendha Lekha, that he would eventually find and strengthen Vinoba Bhave's utopian vision of a truly aware and enlightened system of governance by consensus. In the heart of a region deeply affected by Maoist violence, Mendha Lekha has, over the decades, emerged as an example in the country for tribal communities asserting their right over forests and forest produce.

The tale of Mohan's journey into the jungles, and his partnership with Mendha Lekha's progressive community leader Devaji Tofa, began with that truck ride.

It was the early 1970s. The winds of change were blowing across India. Jayaprakash Narayan's (JP's) clarion call of Sampoorn Kranti—Total Revolution—had roused a generation filled with angst over unemployment and high inflation rates. A massive movement was taking shape in JP's home state of Bihar. The Chhatra Yuva Sangharsh Vahini he had floated was attracting youth from all over India.

In the district of Chandrapur in Maharashtra, Mohan, then in his early twenties, was also impressed with the ideology of the septuagenarian leader. Mohan, too, believed firmly in social justice. His name did not have a surname—only his parents' names—because a surname meant the stamp of caste. He had added his mother's name before his father's to reject patriarchy. Mohan, too, was keen on joining JP's movement and was planning to leave for Bihar. However, he had an equal fascination for the jungles surrounding his hometown and their native inhabitants, the tribals. Mohan wanted to visit Hemalkasa in Gadchiroli, where the legendary social worker Baba Amte had set up the Lok Biradari Prakalp for the integrated development of the Madia Gond tribe. Baba's two sons, Prakash and Vikas, and daughters-in-law, Mandakini and Bharti, were all doctors who served the tribal community. Prakash and Mandakini lived in Hemalkasa, while Vikas, the elder son, along with his wife Bharti, looked after Anandwan, in Warora near Chandrapur, where Baba Amte had established a rehabilitation centre for leprosy patients.

Mohan had met Baba Amte at Anandwan during an event to mark the death anniversary of Sane Guruji, a revered figure in Maharashtra. When Mohan told Baba Amte about his wish to visit Hemalkasa, he was ticked off. 'It is not a picnic spot,' Baba Amte told him. 'Come and stay there for at least a month if you want to learn anything.'

Mohan made up his mind to do so, and his chance came with the truck ride. Dr Vikas Amte used to come to Chandrapur city to ferry people and buy things for both Hemalkasa and Anandwan. Mohan had met him at the Anandwan event. One day, he bumped into Vikas in Chandrapur. He told Vikas that he wanted to visit Hemalkasa. 'Come with me as I am driving there to drop off some groceries and medicines,' said Vikas, offering Mohan a lift in his truck.

It took Mohan barely minutes to go home, pack and inform his parents, two brothers and sister. He was excited. It was the first time that he would be living in the forests, for which he had such a fascination, and meeting the tribals, who intrigued him. It was also the first time he would be leaving the comfort of his home. He left for Hemalkasa on 5 February 1975.

Hemalkasa, in one of India's remotest regions, was an entirely different world. Dr Prakash Amte and his wife, Mandakini, lived like the people they served—in a mud hut. Mohan was given the task of assisting them at the hospital that the couple had set up there. His work included listening to the problems of the tribals who came in for treatment. He began to pick up their language. He learnt about how they lived and the hardships they faced. He also learnt another crucial lesson—how an organization worked for the greater good. Dr Prakash and Dr Mandakini Amte would eventually be conferred the Ramon Magsaysay Award for their work in 2008, and Bill Gates, in 2019, would fete Dr Prakash Amte with a lifetime achievement award from the Indian Council of Medical Research.

The month whizzed by for Mohan. He decided that he needed to stay in Hemalkasa for at least a year. However, JP's call for

Total Revolution still beckoned to him. At the time, attracted by JP's ideology, many young people from across the country had begun to pour into Bihar. At one point, JP announced that there was no need for more people to come. This solved the dilemma in Mohan's mind. He decided to stay back in Hemalkasa. As the year passed, Mohan and a friend, Jagadish Godbole, who shared his room, decided it was time to broaden their horizons. Hemalkasa had given them a glimpse of tribal life and the forests, but it was time to move on.

In 1976, the two friends decided that they would travel along the Indravati river, which flows through Orissa (now Odisha), Chhattisgarh (which was then part of Madhya Pradesh) and Maharashtra. Originating from the ghats—hills—of the Dandakaranya range from the village of Mardiguda in Kalahandi district of Orissa, it courses through Jagdalpur in present Chhattisgarh before merging with the Godavari river near Somnoor in Maharashtra. Throughout its 535-kilometre-long course, the Indravati flows through dense forests of the tribal belt in the three states. The beautiful terrain that it traverses, and the many mythologies surrounding it, add to its allure. It is believed that the river originated when Lord Indra fell in love with a girl named Udanti in a village, leading to his consort, Indrani, becoming a river in grief and cursing Indra and his lover, who became rivers as well. All three rivers—the Indravati, the Indra and the Udanti—flow separately without meeting each other due to Indrani's curse, it is believed. The Indravati becomes a waterfall at Chitrakoot, where, according to Hindu scriptures, Lord Shiva and Parvati came to meet Lord Ram when he, his brother Lakshman and wife Sita had stopped there for a short while.

Mohan's Mohim Indravati—Indravati Initiative—took off with fifteen people. The month-long journey was meticulously planned in advance, including the stops at different villages. The arduous journey, often through dense forests, visiting tribals in their natural surroundings, observing their lifestyle and having campfires under the open skies both satisfied and inflamed Mohan's curiosity about the forests and their inhabitants, both human and animal. The month-long travelling also brought some clarity about the course he should take in the future.

When the group was camping in Jagdalpur, they heard on the radio the news of the Emergency ending and Jayaprakash Narayan asking the youth to set up local chapters of the Chhatra Yuva Sangharsh Vahini wherever they were. He asked them to usher in Total Revolution across the country by mobilizing young people who held no allegiance to any political party. Mohan found his purpose in this. He returned to Chandrapur and started setting up the local chapter of the vahini. He was so involved in the work that, within a year, he had become a core member of JP's vahini at the national level. When the core committee decided that those above thirty years of age should resign, since it was a youth organization, it sparked a lot of opposition. Many asked why they had to quit just when the organization was getting stronger, especially when they had given their entire youth to it. Mohan was present in Patna during the meeting when the disgruntled members of the vahini asked their leader, 'What should we do after leaving this organization that we have nurtured?' In his characteristic way, JP shot back, 'If you still have not figured out what you would do beyond this, *toh aap log sadak khodo* [then dig roads].'

This phrase, '*sadak khodo*', could be interpreted in two ways. One could be: Go indulge in a useless activity such as digging and re-digging roads. The other meaning—the one that Mohan inferred from JP's words—was to go to places that required roads to be built.

Mohan had heard about the tribal socialist leader Sukhadeobabu Uikey, who was fighting for the land rights of his community in Wadsa Desaiganj, on the banks of the Wainganga river in the Gadchiroli region. This was part of the then Chandrapur district. Mohan decided to head there. He and Sukhadeobabu got along very well. They were peas of the same pod in ideology and thought. However, Sukhadeobabu was inclined towards electoral politics. Mohan was averse to it and made it clear. 'If in the future you decide to contest elections, I will neither support nor oppose you,' he told Sukhadeobabu. 'We will just stop working together.'

Sukhadeobabu agreed. He shared Mohan's vision of self-awakening and self-empowerment among the villagers. They decided to work together. Mohan began visiting the villages in and around Wadsa Desaiganj. As soon as he would arrive in a village, the tribal residents would throng around him in the hope that he would provide them with work or other facilities. 'I have not come here to give you jobs or money,' Mohan would tell them. 'What I can do is help you to identify your problems through discussions, and find solutions to them.'

This disappointed many, who stayed away. There were, however, always a few people in the villages who were more aware and had a broader vision. Mohan formed ten study groups, each comprising ten such villagers. They were given a motto: '*Humara rasta hum khud khojenge* [We will find our way ourselves].' The study groups would gather in the evenings at a central place in their villages, and Mohan would encourage them to decide upon a subject for discussion. The first topic the villagers took up was that of minimum wages for farm labour.

Desaiganj was home to tribals as well as non-tribals. The main occupation was farming, and a few big farmers hired labourers to work on their land. For most in the study circles, it was a revelation that minimum wage was their right. Armed with this knowledge, those who laboured in others' farms decided that they would not work unless they were paid minimum wages. An agitation began to brew. The big farmers got a whiff of it. They decided to get workers from neighbouring villages to work on their land instead. When the villagers of Kurud near Wadsa learnt of this, they again held a discussion. A number of options were discussed. Finally, an illiterate woman of the village offered a solution.

When the labourers hired from other villages came, the residents of Kurud welcomed them with garlands. They were offered food and asked to rest. When they were at ease, the hosts explained: 'We understand that you have come here in search of employment, but we are fighting a battle for justice. So we will not let you work.'

In true Gandhian style, the residents told them that they would, instead, go to work on the farms and would give the workers from other villages whatever wages they earned. All of the outsiders returned without doing any work. The victory was a validation of the villagers' motto of finding solutions themselves.

Then Mohan informed the discussion groups about the Employment Guarantee Act of the Maharashtra government. A trade union in the name of Bandhkaam va Lakud Kaamgar Sangathan was registered. Many mainstream trade unions, too, helped Mohan.

From 1979 to 1986, Mohan helped the people of Armori tehsil around Desaiganj fight many such battles for their right to work and livelihood. They learnt to hold agitations armed with weapons of non-violence. With the help of Mohan—who was by now popularly known as Mohan bhau—the villagers prepared extensive documents on the failure of the government machinery to implement the schemes launched for the welfare of tribal and rural labourers. As they became more and more aware of their rights, they held non-violent agitations to press for their demands.

Getting news of the planned agitations, the administration would often issue prohibitory orders and announce that protesters would be breaking the rules and hence would be arrested. The villagers would counter this by asking people to come out and court arrest in large numbers. The police, however, would be wary of making any arrests, because then the reasons for the agitations—failures of the government machinery—would be cited.

The villagers knew that if there was any violence, they would be arrested. So not a single stone was hurled. Nobody came to these agitations drunk. Women always remained at the forefront of such protests. No slogans were shouted against the police. '*Police wala humara bhai hai/Us sey nahi ladai hai* [The police are our brothers/ Our fight is not with them],' they sang. They never demanded the transfer of a serving officer. The fight was with the system, not with the individual serving it.

These agitations also included the massive Jangal Bachao Manav Bachao Andolan, or Save the Forest and Save the People Movement against the government's plan to build two dams—one on the Godavari in Icchampally in Telangana (which was then part of Andhra Pradesh), and the other on the Indravati at Bhopalpatnam on the border of Gadchiroli and Bastar in present-day Chhattisgarh. In the face of a sustained mass movement and protests by the forest-dwelling tribal communities, the government finally had to abandon the projects in 1985.

Sukhadeobabu was also riding the success of these agitations, which empowered the tribal communities and made them aware of their constitutional rights. His popularity was at its peak. He decided to contest in the elections. This was the cue for Mohan to move out of Desaiganj and venture even deeper into the forests.

~

During the movement against the twin dams, two key things happened to Mohan. The first was his marriage to Savita Tare, a master's-degree holder in anthropology and a fellow follower of JP. Savita was from Wardha, but she was also a rebel at heart, who wanted to live for and serve the people who needed help the most and did not want to fit into the traditional role of a *bahu*, or the daughter-in-law of the family.

The other significant thing that happened to Mohan in this period was meeting Devaji Tofa of Mendha Lekha village, the sarpanch of Group Grampanchayat Lekha that had three villages—Mendha, Lekha and Kanardola—as its members.

Around this time, Mohan was reading Gandhi and Vinoba Bhave extensively. He came across a book, *Hind Swaraj,* written by Gandhi in 1908, in which the Mahatma says about the British Parliament,

> 'That which you consider to be the Mother of Parliaments is like a sterile woman and a prostitute. Both these are harsh terms, but exactly fit the case. That Parliament has not yet, of its own accord, done a single good thing. Hence I have compared it to a sterile woman. The natural condition of that Parliament is such that, without outside pressure, it can do nothing. It is

> like a prostitute because it is under the control of ministers who change from time to time.'[2]

Gandhi believed that true power lies with the people and not in the representatives elected by them. In *Hind Swaraj*, he wrote that unless people understood that they had to resolve their issues and learn to make decisions by consensus, a democracy could not be effective.

In 1942, when Vinoba Bhave was incarcerated in Nagpur Jail, he, too, wrote a book, *Swaraj Shastra,* on similar lines. Bhave spoke about *lok shakti*, the power of the people. He evaluated various systems of governance across the globe and advocated for a decision by consensus. Bhave, however, admitted that this was utopian as he had not heard of such a system of governance being practised anywhere. Mohan wanted to venture into that heaven of freedom. He had to learn for himself if such a system—of decision by consensus—was being practised anywhere in the tribal world, the only place it could possibly exist, if it did.

As the movement against the construction of the two dams spread in 1984, Mohan, who was part of the agitation, travelled across villages to create awareness about the ecological imbalances that the dams would create. Tribals from all the villages were coming together, with Devaji Tofa at the forefront of the movement. He would watch Mohan explaining to his people the significance of each and every tree that would be uprooted. 'He would explain the importance of trees such as the mahua and the tendu, and how each and every part of the tree is useful,' Devaji remembers about the early days of his friendship with Mohan.

2 Mahatma Gandhi, *Hind Swaraj or Indian Home-Rule* (Ahmedabad: Navajivan Publishing House, 1938), p. 29, www.mkgandhi.org

'He was speaking about matters that concerned every Adivasi. The way he was explaining it all made me approach him, as there was so much to learn.'

As Mohan moved from village to village with Devaji and another senior tribal resident Faguji Vatti, the discussions veered to other subjects of concern. The region has dense forest cover and a very small portion of land is available for farming. The forest officials had made it clear to the tribals that the forests were the property of the government and taking anything from the jungle would amount to stealing. Mohan and Savita realized that forest rights was the main issue for this community. They decided that in partnership with the *gram* sabha, they would undertake a participatory study-cum-research project on the forests and the tribals living there.

When Mohan spoke about this with Faguji and Devaji, they invited him and his wife to Dhanora tehsil to undertake this study. Mohan laid down certain conditions at the very outset. He told them, 'We will not solve your problems, or give the people employment or money. We will work on the principle of *hum apna rasta khud khojenge* [we'll find our own way]. Those gram sabhas that agree to these conditions can join us for this study and research.'

Sixty-five villages were contacted for the study—twenty-two agreed. Mendha Lekha was one of them.

~

Devaji Tofa, who was born on 20 August 1956, suffered for the ills that plagued tribal society, and that shaped his determination to work for the betterment of his people. His father, a daily-wage labourer, had purchased six acres of land in Mendha from the money he had saved. Like many tribal men of his times, his father, too, brewed liquor and consumed it in large amounts. Devaji had an elder brother who was a daily-wage labourer too. He died of alcoholism. As Mendha did not have a school, Devaji studied in one at a village close by that held classes only up to Class IV. After that, like other boys of the village, Devaji grazed cattle and worked for daily wages.

Devaji, who married a girl of his choice from his village when he was twenty years old, has three children, including two daughters, Manda and Nanda. Both lived in Mendha after they lost their husbands. Devaji, who always wanted his children to be erudite, ensured their education. Manda, who holds a master's degree in social work, is employed with the National Rural Livelihoods Mission. Nanda is a graduate who works with the gram sabha. Devaji's youngest child, Charan Das, is also a graduate and helps manage the work of the gram sabha.

Right from childhood, Devaji took a keen interest in his surroundings. Having seen and suffered for the ill effects of alcoholism among his village and family, he kept away from the bottle. When he was growing up, two things that were extensively discussed in his community were the need for prohibition and forest rights. From the age of sixteen, he began to take part in these discussions. 'I realized that we would have to search for solutions on our own and no government body or organization could get us what we wanted,' remembers Devaji, who now speaks a smattering of English.

The arbitrariness of forest officials was always a cause for worry among forest dwellers, who depended upon the jungles for their livelihood and sustenance. There were always discussions about forest rights. In the early 1980s, a socialist tribal leader and former zamindar of Panabaras from the neighbouring state of present-day Chhattisgarh, Lal Shyamji Maharaj, used to visit the villages in Gadchiroli and hold discussions. Devaji began to attend these meetings. His qualities of being able to grasp the problems and articulate them made him popular in the village. He was appointed a member of the gram panchayat of Mendha from 1979 to 1984, the year he was elected the sarpanch. His leadership has been marked by the ability to take the back seat when things are moving smoothly, and assume charge and lead from the front when the situation demands.

'It would be wrong to call Devaji a village head or a leader as he has never assumed such roles,' says Mohan. 'He has understood the powers that the Indian Constitution vests in its people and encourages his community to understand and utilize that power for their own good.'

Devaji says he has been 'offered election tickets by every political party, but I ask them what more will I get from it that I don't already have or what more would I be able to do?' In fact, he feels that an elected representative tends to move away from the people, while, as the village sarpanch, he has managed to be a hands-on pillar of his community.

When Devaji met Mohan during the anti-dam agitation in 1984, the two connected almost immediately despite their apparent contrast. He was tall and fair, and looked very different from us,' remembers Devaji, who is a little over four feet tall, of Mohan. 'Initially, we all were suspicious. But when we started having discussions, I realized how well read and knowledgeable he was and how well he understood our needs and requirements.'

They had a few things in common too, such as their love for reading, which Mohan inherited from his mother and which

Devaji took refuge in after losing his elder brother to alcoholism. *Gram Geeta*, written by Tukdoji Maharaj, an early-twentieth-century reformer-saint from Maharashtra, had left a deep imprint on Devaji. The book echoes a key Gandhian thought: Uplift of humans is the best way to serve God.

There was a common quest for self-discovery—the belief that their work should not be for but with the people. That is what brought Devaji and Mohan together, as did their sincerity to work for change and the betterment of tribals. Both of them used to commute to twenty-two villages on cycles, and on the way they would discuss various aspects of their work and what had been said by the villagers during the discussion. The discussions would continue over meals that the villagers would offer them. The cultural assimilation was absolute as the two spent long hours together working for their common goals.

'I realized that academics and raw wisdom were two different things,' Mohan says. 'I also observed this during the discussions held at the meets of the study circles.'

As Devaji and Mohan's friendship blossomed, soon the two and elders such as Faguji began to hold conversations on other problems faced by the tribal community. Foremost among them were forest rights and forest management.

~

The relationship between the tribals and the forest department as enforcers of colonial laws such as the Indian Forest Act has traditionally been uneasy and fragile. Tribals were always dependent on forests for their sustenance and livelihood. However, nationalization of the forests altered that relationship. As mentioned earlier, the tribals were told that everything belonged to the government and taking anything out of the forest would amount to stealing, for which they would be arrested and thrown in jail.

Though the residents of Mendha Lekha were unique in taking decisions through consensus, Devaji says, 'They, like other tribals, lived in fear of officials who would often force them to give bribes just to enter the jungles.' The villagers would run and hide in the forest the moment someone of authority, such as the police or forest officials, would visit their area.

The tribals in this region, like other communities, are patriarchal and male-dominated. They did not permit the participation of women in the gram sabha meetings. However, once the importance of women's participation in the fight for forest rights was understood, the male members of the gram sabha approached the women of the village and asked them to participate in the meetings. The women, grappling with and suffering from the results of rampant alcoholism, put forth the condition that for them to get involved in the working of the gram sabha, this issue had to be taken up. Alcohol consumption and its ill effects were discussed for nearly one and a half years in the study circles that Mohan set up. The gram sabha decided to ban liquor, but in a limited way. It would not be made or sold in the village. It would be made and distributed only for rituals such as weddings and births, and women would decide the quantity. The gram sabha's approval would be a must for personal consumption.

Devaji took a keen interest in these initiatives. He would also accompany Mohan to other villages and learn through the meetings being held there. Mohan's study circles had expanded.

By 1989, discussions about traditional forest rights, also known as nistar rights, were being held in earnest at Mendha Lekha. The villagers decided to try to locate the original nistar documents related to their village and forests. Devaji, along with fellow villagers, began to visit the revenue department. After great difficulty and sustained efforts, they succeeded in locating the documents pertaining to their nistar rights over land in village and forests. The villagers came to know that they had rights over 1,800.07 hectares of forest. If they used anything from that area for their consumption, they would not be stealing and hence would not be liable for any punishment.

Armed with this knowledge, they began to conduct many Gandhian agitations, such as putting to test their nistar rights for construction of a *ghotul*—the tribal society's equivalent of a club, where young men and women hang out. It is a circular, hut-like structure made with wood and mud, where young boys and girls of the village gather in the evenings to exchange ideas, and enjoy art performances and games. The boys and girls also spend the night there, and the ghotul is where many marriages are fixed. It is strictly for single men and women, and out of bounds for the elderly and the married.

The gatherings at ghotuls, long an ancient tribal custom, were, however, gradually disappearing. For the tribals, a ghotul is more like a centre of tribal culture—nothing taught in a school can match the experiences and learnings from a ghotul. But these clubs were being targeted as immoral places of lust. 'School education, which had come to these tribal villages, was creating an urge among the tribal youth to be more like the urban crowd. They were beginning to find most of their own customs primitive,' Mohan remembers.

In Mendha, there was an earnest discussion on whether a ghotul made of teak wood should be constructed in the village without the permission of the forest department. Use of teak wood was not permitted even during the days of the zamindari system. Chopping of teak invited a hefty fine and even a jail term. The villagers were of the opinion that the requirement was for a traditional purpose, so it should be permissible. Finally, the women reasoned that this would put to test if they really had nistar rights. The villagers decided that their protest would be peaceful even if the authorities took action. They would test their rights as a community, but by staying united and non-violent.

On the decided date in December, the villagers gathered in the forest. The teak wood for the ghotul was cut and carried to the village. The forest officials were aware of this development. The first to visit the village was a forest guard, who asked them the reason for chopping the wood. He was told that it would be used for constructing a ghotul. Then the forest ranger arrived. If the wood was not surrendered, it would be forcibly confiscated, he warned. The villagers heard him out but did not relent. Finally, a mobile forest court arrived in Mendha. The villagers told the officials the reason for collecting the wood and also that if it was taken away forcibly, they would hold a peaceful agitation. The court returned without being able to solve the impasse. Aware that the wood would soon be taken away, the entire village worked through the night, and by the next morning the ghotul was ready.

On 3 January 1990, more than 400 armed policemen reached Mendha to assist the forest officials. Gadchiroli being the heart of the Maoist insurgency in the region, there were always armed personnel ready. The force found that all the women of Mendha were sitting in the ghotul and singing traditional songs. The villagers, who knew that the armed officials were coming, had deployed their most Gandhian defence.

The cops ordered the women to vacate the ghotul. The women answered that it was a traditional structure and that they had used their nistar rights to take the wood and construct it. The cops told the women that the wood had been stolen from the jungle and that made it an illegal structure, which they were going to pull down.

'Who are you to decide that the structure is illegal?' retorted Vimlabai Usendi, one of the women in the ghotul, who was a member of the gram panchayat. 'It is the court that will take this decision. Ask the forest officials to go to court.'

Not expecting such a knowledgeable response, the cops were taken aback. However, they told the women that they were there to protect the forest officials and if the women obstructed their work, the police would have to use force. Coolly, the women retorted that they would not come in the way of the officials, but if the ghotul was pulled down, the villagers would go to the forest the next day and chop more wood to build it again. The cops ignored it as an empty threat. The ghotul was pulled down, the wood confiscated and carried away by the forest officials.

The villagers returned to the jungle, chopped down more wood and built another ghotul overnight. They had already written a letter to the district collector informing him about the significance of the ghotul and how they had only used their nistar rights to collect wood for building the traditional structure.

The news that cops and forest officials had forcibly destroyed the ghotul in Mendha Lekha spread like fire among the Gond tribals. Though ghotuls had disappeared from most of the villages, they knew its traditional significance. There was widespread anger over the police action. A panchayat meeting was called in Dhanora tehsil. Devaji Tofa was present at the meeting. He told the members that the tribals had no power outside their villages. Any protest would be dealt with by the administration with a heavy hand. He cited the example of a fish out of water—it would be helpless and struggle to survive. His suggestion was that if any action were to be taken, it be in the villages, where the unity of the people was their strength. Devaji said that the other villages should also use their nistar rights to gather wood and construct ghotuls. In a week's time, twelve ghotuls were ready in as many villages.

The administration was stumped. The officials realized that if pulling down one ghotul resulted in a dozen springing up, pulling down the new ones would only aggravate the situation further. The district collector called a meeting of senior officials, in which it was agreed that building a ghotul was a traditional right of the tribal community. If they used their nistar rights in the forest to collect wood for this purpose, the forest officials should have no objection. The government also decided to build these structures in tribal villages, albeit with concrete.

The ghotul in Mendha Lekha was inaugurated on 26 January 1990 in the presence of district officials.

~

By the beginning of the 1990s, the forest department in Maharashtra had started the process of creating reserve forests in the area, which had come under its jurisdiction in 1951 after the end of the zamindari system. This posed a challenge for Mendha Lekha, as out of its 1,800 hectares of forest, nistar rights would be applicable to only 500 hectares; the remaining would come under reserve forest. The study circles began to discuss solutions to this problem.

Mohan informed them about the joint forest management programme of the Maharashtra government. Mendha Lekha sent an application expressing its desire to be part of this scheme. From 1992 to 2008, the village worked under the joint forest management scheme. This way the villagers could save their nistar rights over the 1,800 hectare jungle even though it was part of a reserve forest.

In 2006, the Indian government introduced the new Forest Rights Act. This was significant as, besides the tribals' rights under nistar, the new law would give the villagers ownership rights on minor forest produce, and grazing and management rights over forests—including their timber and water. The law vested these rights in the villagers, but they had to claim it by presenting the relevant documents.

Forest rights committees began to be formed in villages across the state. Mendha Lekha preferred to make a collective claim first, instead of individual rights. To make such a claim, the documents that were needed were the nistar records, the map of the village as per the records of the revenue department and a map of the jungle under the boundaries of the village, in accordance with the records of the forest department. Any error in any of these documents would result in the claim being rejected.

Mendha Lekha took the smart way out. The village asked the administration to check these documents in their own records. The local administration agreed to provide these documents to the forest rights committee. The initiative taken by Mendha Lekha helped the rest of the villages in the district to follow the same procedure to obtain their forest rights. Mendha Lekha's claim was accepted, and it was given forest rights over 1,800.7 hectares. The declaration was made on 15 August 2009—fittingly, Independence Day—by the district collector and the minister in charge of the district of Gadchiroli.

This was a historic moment—Mendha Lekha became the first village in the country to get community forest resources under the Forest Rights Act that came into force in 2008. This marked the culmination of a thirty-year fight for rights, and also the end of decades of injustice that the tribal community had suffered.

The struggle, however, was not over. The forest department contended that bamboo was a tree and so was not a 'minor' forest produce that the village had rights over. Though the villagers could sell bamboo, the buyer was required to carry a transit pass issued by forest officials. The officials would refuse to issue this pass to any buyer. Thus began another round of tussles with the forest department for the issuance of the transit passes. Team Mendha Lekha kept up the pressure. It was decided that one member from each family would go to the forest and get a single bamboo. He would take the main road leading to the village and give it to the depot set up in the village for this purpose. The gram sabha would sell only one bamboo to one person, and the buyer would pay for it, collect a receipt and demand a transit pass from the forest department. 'This was on the lines of the salt satyagraha that Gandhi had carried out at Dandi during the freedom movement,' says Mohan. Eventually, the department relented after much goading and instructions from the Union government in New Delhi.

On 27 April 2011, Mendha Lekha became the first village in the country to get the rights to issue transit passes for bamboo. Its ownership of its forests was now complete and absolute. Devaji Tofa had achieved for his village what his community thought was impossible. Mohan's efforts in empowering the tribal community had shown remarkable results.

Mohan had creatively helped the gram sabha utilize laws that were beneficial to the villagers, to set them on the quest for Swarajya, or self-rule. Through the study circles where the villagers would meet and discuss issues that affected their lives, Mohan had taught them to find solutions. His efforts were recognized in 2016, when he was presented the prestigious Jamnalal Bajaj Award for Constructive Work.

~

Mendha Lekha is located 30 kilometres from the headquarters of Gadchiroli district, a known hotbed of Maoist violence. Ninety per cent of the village is forest area. The large varieties of produce from the forest include bamboo, mahua, tendu leaf, chironji (*Buchanania lanzan*), gum and teak wood. The way the villagers have protected and nurtured the deciduous forest is what makes Mendha Lekha unique.

'We elect the government at the Centre and state, but in our village we are the government,' is the motto of the village. With neatly lined thatched-roof houses and toilets in every home, Mendha Lekha stands out from other villages. The gram sabha building is located under a cluster of huge trees, in the shade of which large cement platforms have been built. It is here that the members of the gram sabha meet—to discuss, debate and decide. Facing the gram sabha is a huge door made of heavy teak wood with tribal motifs etched on it. It leads to a spacious community centre, where the village head meets people who come to study its unique style of functioning.

Over the years, when the residents of Mendha Lekha would discuss how to strengthen the gram sabha, one subject that would come up frequently was of Gramdan—collective land ownership of the village, which had its roots in Vinoba Bhave's Gramdan Movement.

Bhave had started the Bhoodan Movement in 1951 in his quest for a classless society and to empower the landless. The movement was for the transfer of land from landowners, who held big swathes, to the landless. Bhave himself, however, was not satisfied. He realized that this movement could make the landless farmer an owner of land, but the system of individual land holdings would not change. He felt that land is a productive resource and not a product that can be bought and sold. This became the genesis of the Gramdan Movement. Under this, the owner of the land would voluntarily transfer his land in the name of the gram sabha. The entire land in a village would thus be in the name of the gram sabha and there would be no individual land holdings. This would make the entire village one family. The Maharashtra Gramdan Act, 1964, was an outcome of this movement. Initially, nineteen villages in the state had implemented some provisions of the Act, but later it was all but forgotten.

According to Devaji, the Gond tribals do not traditionally see land as property or something to be owned by individuals. The community views it as a collective resource, and believes that with private ownership, people tend to get selfish and isolated. 'Over the years, however, a cultural change had gradually seeped in,' says Mohan. 'The desire for individual property rights had taken root in tribal communities too.' At the study circle meetings, the villagers discussed the advantages of collective ownership. These included more autonomy to the gram sabha and protection of the land from being grabbed by outsiders. They realized that it was more beneficial to the community as well as to the individual if the ownership of land was collective and not private. This would also further strengthen the gram sabha.

The entire village had to agree before this could be implemented. Many could refuse to part with the land that belonged to their ancestors. So the gram sabha decided that those in the age group of fourteen to eighteen years would also be consulted—so that in the future they may not contest the decision or have regrets about it. Devaji Tofa's wise words made an impact on his community. He told them, 'Believe in yourself. If you stand by the decisions taken by consensus in the *gaon samaj sabha* (village council), it will be for your good and the good of our village.'

In 2013, with a representative of the district administration present, the gram sabha unanimously passed the resolution that fifty-two families of the village would donate 200 hectares of land owned by them to the gram sabha. This turned Mendha Lekha into a single family. It was declared the first Gramdan village in thirty-five years. The announcement was published in the *Gazette of Government of Maharashtra* the same year.

Mohan Hirabai Hiralal was the architect of this revolutionary change. The power and wisdom of the villagers, and the dynamic leadership of Devaji Tofa, too, played a key role in taking the community towards *poorna swaraj*—the vision of self-sufficient villages espoused by Mahatma Gandhi, Vinoba Bhave and their ideological heirs, including JP.

'Mendha Lekha showed the world that governing by consensus was not a utopian concept. It was workable if supported by the study circle as a separate structure than the decision-making gram sabha, and if the values of equity and non-violence were accepted,' says Mohan. 'In this world in the grips of violence, terrorism, exploitation, fear and insecurities, Mendha Lekha has proved that Sarvodaya and Swarajya are not merely utopian concepts, but can be applied and implemented at village and local levels by the people themselves.'

Digant and Anagha, Aniket and Samiksha Amte

KEEPERS OF THE FLAME

Digant and Aniket Amte had no idea how extraordinary their lives were.

Their earliest childhood memory was of living in a mud hut in Hemalkasa, a small village in Bhamragarh taluka of Maharashtra's Gadchiroli district, surrounded by thick forests and four rivers—Indravati, Godavari, Wainganga and Pranhita.

When Digant and Aniket's parents, Dr Prakash and Dr Mandakini Amte, arrived to serve the Madia Gond tribal community here in the early 1970s, there was no electricity, roads or any such sign of civilization for hundreds of kilometres in any direction. Even now, the drive to Hemalkasa, 200 kilometres from the nearest city of Chandrapur, is through thick forest. Tall trees line both sides of the road, with greenery as far as the eye can see. The way is often narrow and dotted with signboards that warn vehicles to slow down to allow wild animals to cross. Famous for its bamboo and teak, the forests are the traditional home of the Gond and Madia tribes.

The jungles have thinned now and the wildlife, too, has dwindled, but when Digant and Aniket were growing up, the forests that Hemalkasa is nestled in were very dense. The brothers would spend hours climbing trees, looking for different species of birds and animals, and swimming in the rivers with their friends. They went to the same school as the tribal children, who were the only friends they had. The brothers also picked up Madia, the local language.

For them, this was the only way to live. They didn't know any other way of life to compare this with. The world would discover Hemalkasa much later. Until the early 1990s, very few people knew about the work the Amte family was doing. When Digant and Aniket were growing up, there were never any visitors—not even relatives. Three to four times a year a truck would come with groceries and medicines for the hospital that Digant and Aniket's parents ran. Innocent and carefree—that's how they remember growing up. They would see their parents attending to patients—mostly stung by insects, bitten or mauled by wild beasts or suffering from debilitating diseases. At that time, the significance of their work was lost on the young boys. That their parents had come voluntarily to one of the remotest regions of the country to serve an extremely impoverished and neglected population was something that would dawn on them much later, when they would head to cities to pursue their higher education.

Digant and Aniket are grandsons of Baba Amte, a well-known messiah for the most impoverished, who set up the Lok Biradari Prakalp in Hemalkasa in December 1973. Baba Amte, who hailed from an extremely wealthy family of landowners in Wardha district, had studied to become a lawyer but his heart lay in service to those most in need and those most spurned by society. Baba Amte had lived in Sevagram in Wardha, the ashram where Mahatma Gandhi stayed, and was his ardent follower. He set up a hospital for leprosy patients at Anandwan near Warora in 1949, and two other facilities for the disabled and the marginalized people of the society under the auspices of the Maharogi Sewa Samiti. His two sons, the elder Vikas and the younger Prakash, are both doctors and have carried forward the work started by their illustrious father. Prakash and his doctor wife, Mandakini, came to Hemalkasa in 1974, the same year they got married. They set up their clinic in a bamboo hut and began to treat patients. Their elder son, Digant, was born on 9 August 1975. Aniket was born two years later, on 6 August 1977.

Initially, the local population was indifferent to the family's efforts to provide medical facilities to them. Prakash and Mandakini, however, followed Baba Amte's philosophy—that work should never be *for* the people but *with* the people. They engaged with the tribal community not as a service, but worked with them to improve the conditions.

There was a government school in Bhamragarh, but it did not have too many students. The staff seldom reported for duty and none of the students had gone beyond Class IV. In 1976, Dr Prakash Amte set up the Lok Biradari Prakalp Ashramshala, a residential school, near his hospital. A few of his friends volunteered to teach the students. The school started with a kindergarten section and Class I. Then on, a class was added each year. When it was Digant and Aniket's turn to head to school, it had 330 children—almost all tribal—from neighbouring villages. The Amte boys also got admission in this ashramshala.

When Digant turned nine, he was sent to Anandwan, where the Amtes' project had grown phenomenally by the turn of the decade. The school had expanded and Anandwan had its own college. Aniket, too, went there, but at the age of thirteen. They were hit with the pangs of growing up, of being separated from their parents and the idyllic life of Hemalkasa. The boys would return home during festivals and holidays. By now, there was a steady stream of volunteers, who would visit Hemalkasa to work in the school and hospital. The initial quiet that surrounded the campus had been replaced with bustling activity, and the boys enjoyed it.

Prakash and Mandakini had set up a community kitchen, where meals were cooked for the residential students, volunteers and the patients who would come for treatment from far-flung villages. The Amte family, too, ate their meals here. Mandakini, along with the wives of volunteers and some local help, prepared the food, and everybody would sit and eat together. Big festivals such as Diwali and Ganesh Utsav were special occasions when prasad and *falhar*—sweet and savoury snacks—were prepared for all. All celebrations would be in one place, where everybody gathered to have fun. It was one big, happy family, Digant and Aniket remember. They also remember going on picnics on Sundays and holidays together. They would head to the riverside, where the women cooked on open fires. The kids would bathe in the river and frolic around until sunset.

After clearing his Class XII board exams from Anandwan, Digant studied medicine at the Jawaharlal Nehru Medical College in Wardha. About 310 kilometres from Hemalkasa and its balmy calm, it was at the medical school that Digant was hit by the full import of how different their lives actually were. Some of his professors at the medical college had been classmates of his parents and were kind to him, but mostly he did not speak about life in Hemalkasa or the work his parents were doing. Two years later, Aniket decided he did not wish to study medicine. He took a diploma in mechanical engineering at Dyaneshwar Vidyapeeth in Pune, a buzzing metropolitan city that was completely different from the quiet, remote Hemalkasa and Anandwan.

Digant and Aniket could not fit in. They were not used to the parties their peers would frequently throw or attend. Both kept away, one reason for which was that their parents used to work for a small honorarium of Rs 500 per month. They could barely afford the cost of educating their children in the cities. Digant and Aniket never had any money to splurge. Both brothers understood the efforts their parents were making to educate them, and also in serving the people of Hemalkasa. The cities, with beggars on the roads and rampant crime, were as unlike the tribal idylls of their village as could be.

The concept of locking up homes did not exist in Hemalkasa. The tribals never locked their homes. But in the hostels, both brothers had to keep their belongings under constant lock and key for fear of things being stolen. Both brothers mostly kept to themselves and were always eager to get back home. As the name of the Amtes spread across Maharashtra and the world, many of Digant and Aniket's peers sneered at them that the family was only in it for name and fame. It was like being trolled, but to their faces as opposed to these days on social media.

None of their friends ever showed any eagerness to visit their home to understand the work the Amtes were doing. The brothers withdrew deeper within themselves and kept away from company. Their only aim was to complete their education and return home to Hemalkasa. Digant did two house jobs in general surgery and orthopaedics after completing his MBBS. He returned to Hemalkasa in 1999 and joined his parents at the hospital. Three years later, Aniket, too, returned to the forests, his tribal friends and the scores of animals his father had rescued.

~

Hunting used to be the main occupation of the tribal community. They would hunt anything that moved in the jungles, as it was their food. In the early days, when Dr Prakash Amte started his work at Hemalkasa, he would often see tribal men carrying a dead monkey or deer, its limbs tied to a bamboo pole. The prevalent practice was to kill the young ones of these animals, too, if they were around. This alarmed Prakash, because there was a threat of many species being wiped out. One day when he saw a tribal man walking with a bamboo stick on which a monkey and its baby were hanging, he stopped the man and told him not to kill the baby. He offered to take the baby and, in return, said he would give the man some grain or rotis. Eager for rice or roti, the tribals started bringing to the Amte campus the orphaned offspring of the animals they had hunted. All the offspring were taken care of—most of them spent their entire lives at what later came to be known as Amte's Ark.

Many wild beasts—including leopards, tigers, bears, deer, porcupines, squirrels, eagles and owls—were given shelter at the ark. Aniket was extremely fond of many of these animals. Once back at Hemalkasa, he took up the work of expanding their cages. He also took up administrative work at the office and school run by Lok Biradari Prakalp, the social project of Maharogi Sewa Samiti, which had been set up by his grandfather, the visionary Baba Amte.

Meanwhile, a search was on to find a bride for the tall and good-looking Dr Digant Amte, but it was largely drawing a blank because not too many parents were keen on their daughters starting a new life in the jungles. One evening, however, Dr Prakash Amte got a call from a man in Goa, who introduced himself as Kamlakar Sadhale. He said that he was an architect and that his daughter, Anagha, who was also a doctor, had gone through his son's bio data (received from one of their friends). She was keen to take things forward. Sadhale, his son and daughter-in-law were all architects in Goa. The family had also established an environmental organization, so Anagha had an idea of what social work entailed.

The phone call stirred up much excitement in the Amte house. The discussions veered from 'how long will a girl from Goa live here in this jungle?' to 'she is attracted to the romanticism of it ... she will realize that it's not easy and will give up'. However, a meeting was set up. Considering the distance between Hemalkasa and Goa, it was decided that the two would meet in Pune, at the home of a relative of Vilas Manohar, who had been serving in Hemalkasa with the Amtes for a long time.

At an apartment in an upper-middle-class locality of Pune, Digant told his prospective wife about the difficulties that she could face in Hemalkasa. 'There is no electricity there, no market to shop in. The nearest city is Chandrapur, 200 kilometres away. Telephone connectivity is feeble, and friends and relatives find it difficult to visit the place.' He told her that there would be no evenings out to a cinema or to restaurants, as there were none there. He also told her that she should not have any expectations of earning a decent salary in lieu of the hard work and long hours she would have to put in at the hospital. She would be paid a paltry amount as honorarium. 'And don't expect any gratitude for what you will do for the people there. It is not that we are serving them. This work is being done because we enjoy it,' he told her.

Anagha did not flinch—she was made of sterner stuff. After graduating from Goa Medical College, she had taken up a job in a corporate hospital. The highly commercialized environment convinced her that this was not how she wanted to practise her profession. Once, she delivered the baby of the daughter-in-law of a diamond merchant. The woman then demanded that a gynaecologist and a paediatrician stand beside her whenever she had to feed her baby. Anagha had vowed that she would never take up a job that involved such humiliation for the doctor. To her, the dedication of the Amtes was a virtue, not a hurdle.

When the Sadhales arrived at the sprawling yet spartan residence of Prakash and Mandakini Amte, they found the situation much better than what they were prepared for. The long journey had sapped them of energy, but the peaceful environment and the natural beauty appealed to the family of architects.

The marriage of Prakash Amte's elder son was solemnized on 28 September 2003 in Anandwan. That was the year Baba Amte turned ninety years old. The wedding saw a reunion of his old friends, relatives and associates. Thousands were present to bless the newly-weds. This included more than 1,000 volunteers of the Lok Biradari Prakalp and Anandwan, and the 2,000 leprosy patients who had been treated and rehabilitated by the Amte family.

Soon after the wedding, the family returned to Hemalkasa with its newest member. Digant and his wife almost immediately began work at the hospital. Anagha, being a gynaecologist, filled a long-standing need at the hospital. She introduced Caesarean sections for difficult deliveries. Tribal women rely on midwives who assist them in childbirth at home. Realizing that such practices exposed these women to immense risk, Dr Anagha Amte began to work closely with expectant mothers and earned their confidence. She could persuade many to opt for hospital deliveries. This resulted in a sharp decline in infant mortality, especially among babies with low birthweight.

She also worked to promote hygiene among tribal women by introducing them to clean practices during menstruation. For this she was awarded the Sakhi SHERO award by the Vatsalya Foundation in 2018.

~

While Dr Digant and Dr Anagha Amte were taking the hospital's work forward, Aniket Amte began to organize the administrative side of the Lok Biradari Prakalp. The first thing on his agenda was to start Classes XI and XII at the school. It was also important to spread the word about the work being done here. But the most pressing concern was to get the required funds to continue with the numerous projects that he hoped to introduce.

The services at the hospital, including medicines, are free and no charges are collected from the patients even for food. At the school as well, the children do not pay any fees or hostel charges. Uniforms, books and stationery are also provided free of cost. A government grant provides for 450 students, but the current number enrolled was 650.

When Digant and Aniket began work at Hemalkasa, the big task before them was to improve the existing infrastructure. The small structures that housed the hospital and the school were built during the time of Baba Amte. At that time, there were no funds and no resources to transport the building material. The small buildings and houses back then were made with mud bricks baked in a kiln set up on the premises. Layers of mud were put between the bricks to keep them together. Wood was used for the ceiling and to make pillars. Termites thrive in the forest areas of Hemalkasa, and more so in houses made of mud. They had eaten into Hemalkasa's structures over four decades.

Digant and Aniket also felt the need to improve the infrastructure and make it ready for the youngsters who were now going there to do voluntary work. Most of them were from big cities. Aniket understood that they would need better living quarters and a comfortable stay in Hemalkasa. The brothers decided that they not only had to reconstruct the existing buildings but also add to them to accommodate the increasing number of patients in the hospital and students in the school. All this was, of course, easier to decide than execute. Aniket had to juggle funds and cut costs to make ends meet as they expanded the facilities.

The media boom in the 1990s and the Magsaysay Award presented to Dr Prakash and Dr Mandakini Amte in 2008 put Hemalkasa in the spotlight. Awareness about the work being done in Hemalkasa increased exponentially. They were written about more and their visibility on electronic media increased. But the media glare also brought misconceptions. Aniket continued to draw a blank whenever he asked for discounts for bulk purchases of goods and materials. He would tell the vendors that the purchases were for community welfare projects. The facilities they were providing were free of cost, so a bit of a discount would go a long way in helping them meet their expenses. 'Money? Money is no problem for you. There is so much foreign funding coming in,' Aniket would be told. But the requirement for funds was so omnipresent, urgent and immediate that he never got tired of asking for concessions wherever possible.

He also realized their work could progress best when people saw and understood it first-hand. To create awareness about Hemalkasa, he designed photo and handicraft exhibitions. He took these events to cities such as Nagpur, Hyderabad and Pune—to disseminate information about the Lok Biradari Prakalp and also to attract volunteers to work here. That is how he found his life partner too.

~

Samiksha Godse first arrived in Hemalkasa in 2007 as a volunteer who had recently completed her master's degree in economics.

Samiksha, the only child of her parents, was born and brought up in Pune. She was always happy, carefree and willing to explore the unknown. She dabbled in theatre, hung out with friends and went for movies. She loved the city life. After completing her post-graduation, she was still figuring out her future when the idea of working as a volunteer at Hemalkasa caught her attention. She discussed it with a friend. They decided to travel around the state and make Hemalkasa part of the trip. They visited the Konkan region first, followed by Bhamragarh.

Aniket was not there when Samiksha reached Hemalkasa with her friend. Both stayed at the Lok Biradari Prakalp for three days and familiarized themselves with the place. On her way back to Pune, she met Aniket in Nagpur. 'It was a very formal meeting and we discussed my experiences at Hemalkasa. That was all. From Nagpur I took a bus back to Pune,' she recalls. Hemalkasa was just a place she had visited. Once back in Pune, she ticked it off her 'to-do' list.

After a couple of months, Aniket was in Pune with an exhibition. Samiksha heard of it and visited the venue. The two caught up again and discussed Hemalkasa and the work being done there. Over the next year, they kept meeting at various venues. Neither realized that they were getting closer or falling in love. 'I will not be able to pinpoint at what juncture we decided that we are made for each other,' she says.

Once they realized that they wanted to spend their life together, they told their parents. The Amtes were fine with it, but Samiksha's parents were not too eager. The long distance and the remoteness of Hemalkasa troubled them. 'You were born and brought up in Pune,' Samiksha's father, a corporate-sector employee, reasoned with her. 'You are used to the trappings of a big city. Do you realize how lonely and monotonous life will be at Hemalkasa?'

He didn't realize that his daughter had already gone over these doubts in her mind and had even discussed them with Aniket. Samiksha was convinced that this was the life she wanted to live. Soon, she was able to convince her parents too. Aniket and Samiksha got married on 19 December 2008 in Anandwan.

~

When she arrived again in Hemalkasa, this time as a bride, Samiksha began to figure out her role there. It took her one year to decide that she would take up the functioning of the school. Gradually she began to understand how it worked and what was needed to make it better.

So far, the medium of instruction in the school had been Marathi, which was not the local language. The tribal children spoke Madia but their textbooks were in Marathi, the state language.

'I could see that the children were not being able to relate to the subjects being taught in a language they did not fully comprehend,' Samiksha remembers. 'This was coming in the way of more interactive learning. The children who spoke Madia found it difficult to cope with Marathi or Hindi.'

Samiksha believes children develop cognitive skills better when they are initially taught in their mother tongue. With that in mind, she began to devise a multilingual education programme in accordance with the Right of Children to Free and Compulsory Education Act, 2009. Under this module, the kindergarten students were taught only in their mother tongue, Madia. They were introduced to the Devanagari script in a very limited way. The learning tools, too, included things they were familiar with. By the time the children reached Class I, Samiksha found that they could understand the script—which is the same for Hindi and Marathi—and were ready to learn in Marathi. Samiksha also felt the need to introduce the English language. The school is partly English-medium now.

By 2014, the birth centenary year of Baba Amte, six years after his passing, Digant and Aniket had made major additions to the hospital and the school in Hemalkasa. They arranged for funds to construct a neonatal intensive care unit, an ICU, three major operation theatres, another separate operation theatre for eye surgery, wards and delivery rooms. The hospital now provides treatment to 35,000 patients every year.

The school in Hemalkasa has twenty-five teachers and some of the appointments are made through the state's tribal welfare department. The school has had a makeover too, with more dormitories and a computer lab with forty computers. Information technology companies donated the first computers but they were old, overused machines and did not last long. Aniket raised funds and bought new machines. Now tribal students browse national and international news, learn about new trends, and study and gather more information about themselves online—just like their peers in faraway cities. Their quest for information has made them more aware of the fragility of their idyllic surroundings. This shows in the essays that they write on topics related to the environment, where they express their anguish over the large-scale hunting of animals by their ancestors.

A large number of tribal men look after the animals at the ark too. Most arrived here as babies and were never released back into the jungles even when they grew up. These animals, unknown to the ways of the wild, would have perished if not sheltered by the Amtes. They are fed and looked after by human beings, and are not scared of men. As most wild animals have a lifespan of around fifteen years, they have continued to live at the ark and are an attraction for the children who stay and study here.

The school has groomed many bright students, who are now doctors, engineers, in government service, in the police and the forest departments. Many former students also work as teachers or volunteers. The fourth generation of the Amtes, Digant's sons Arnav and Ahaan, and Aniket's son Nirzar and daughter Rumani, are also studying here.

Every year the school takes in fifty-five students in Class I, and the seats are filled up in minutes. Both Aniket and Samiksha feel sorry that they are not able to accommodate more students. The children are selected on the basis of distance—those from far away are given preference as it is a residential school.

Aniket was besieged with demands from the tribal community living in the more far-flung parts to set up a school for them closer to their homes. The Amtes finally gave in and decided in 2015 to set up a school in Nelgunda, 27 kilometres into the forests from Hemalkasa. There is no proper road to Nelgunda and the electricity supply is erratic.

This is the heart of the jungle terrain, where the Indian state is at war with Maoist guerrillas. Nelgunda has witnessed a lot of bloodshed over the years. Skirmishes between the insurgents and police are common. The place is dangerously close to the Naxal headquarters of Abujhmad. The school here run by the district administration, is nearly defunct.

Initially, Aniket had requested the government to allow them to run the zilla parishad school, but the proposal was rejected. Not willing to disappoint the villagers who had approached them with such hope, Aniket and Samiksha then decided to set up their own school. A villager, Malu Warse, agreed to give them two acres of barren land he owned, on a monthly rent of Rs 2,000. The school, named Sadhana Vidyalaya after Baba Amte's wife, opened on 5 May 2015 in a small shed with fifty-two children in kindergarten, and Classes I and II. The children were from eight villages that surrounded the area.

Attending school every day was tough for the students, who were all below ten years of age. Most of them would walk 5 kilometres through thick forests and cross a shallow river to reach Nelgunda. Once again, Dr Prakash and Dr Mandakini Amte relied on their band of dedicated volunteers to fill in as teachers. Besides them, three local tribal youths are also associated with the school and take classes.

The institution has been a big hit with the children of the surrounding villages. Samiksha devised a method that makes learning fun and participatory, and made English the medium of instruction. To everyone's surprise, the children picked up the language very quickly.

In six years, the school strength has grown to 150 children. Even though they have got no government grant or aid, the Amtes have been adding classes, and the school is now up to Class V. However, the school still faces what seem like insurmountable odds. During the rains it becomes inaccessible and remains closed from 1 July to 15 September. The school provides bicycles to children during the winter months to make their commute easier.

The tribal community has welcomed the school, Samiksha says. The community has seen the success of those who are in government jobs, thanks to their education. The Amtes have won the tribal communities' trust through decades of service. People now come willingly to the hospital, unlike four decades ago, when they were sceptical. Such is the faith in the father and son serving here that the local patients ask for treatment in only Hemalkasa, and are wary of going elsewhere. Their appearance, poverty and the language barrier all add to their reluctance to go to cities for treatment.

The hospital in Hemalkasa organizes three surgical camps in a year. Doctors from the cities come to treat patients who require help from specialists. The widespread use and consumption of tobacco in the region is responsible for the large number of oral cancer patients here. Digant has tied up with the dental college at Sawangi in Wardha, where he refers these patients who are provided the treatment free of charge. Otherwise it would cost them hundreds of thousands of rupees.

Government infrastructure in the backward tribal regions of Gadchiroli was ramped up in the first decade of the twenty-first century. Zilla parishad schools and hostels opened up, and primary healthcare centres were set up. However, the number of patients coming to the Amtes' hospital or students coming for enrolment in the schools run by the Lok Biradari Prakalp has never shown any decline. Doctors at government set-ups and teachers at state-run schools are often reluctant to serve under these harsh conditions. For the Amtes, it's a labour of love.

Dr Prakash and Dr Mandakini Amte stopped seeing patients a few years back. Now Dr Digant and Dr Anagha Amte are in charge of the hospital. They continue to get patients from as far as 200 kilometres from Hemalkasa. It disturbs Digant and he takes no pride in it. 'To reach here, a patient definitely crosses at least two to three primary healthcare centres,' he explains. 'That the patient still comes here even for minor ailments shows that he does not get the required service at government hospitals.'

The ambience in the Hemalkasa hospital is very different from such facilities in cities, where relatives of patients beating up doctors is common, if not rampant. In Hemalkasa, Dr Digant and Dr Anagha Amte enjoy the complete trust and faith of their patients—just like Digant's parents did. The hospital takes no government support, except for some surgeries, which are now reimbursed under the health insurance schemes of the government.

The many infrastructural and administrative changes that the two have brought about have given the Lok Biradari Prakalp a modern look. Their constant effort is to be able to sustain the initiatives that their grandfather and parents started.

The 45-acre campus is now dotted with modern buildings and living quarters. Buses parked outside the campus bring in a steady stream of visitors from across the state who come here to see and understand the work.

The brothers don't let the burden of their legacy bog them down. 'It would be okay if people say that we are not as good as our parents or grandparents, but it would be terrible if they were to say that we brought down the family name,' says Aniket.

The brothers do get their share of flak, especially from the associates of their illustrious grandfather. The elderly have reservations about the reconstruction of original structures built by Baba Amte. 'You come here for a day or two but we work here and have to accommodate the ever-rising number of people who visit the hospital and study in the school,' Digant and Aniket reason with the grumpy friends of Baba Amte.

On Sundays, Digant's sons play cricket on the concrete footpaths that surround the numerous buildings. Having been separated from the comforts of home at a very young age, when he was sent to Anandwan, Digant wants to keep his children in Hemalkasa until they finish Class X.

Just as Prakash and Mandakini had voluntarily come here to serve the underprivileged, Aniket and Digant, too, never considered any option other than Hemalkasa. They are here because they enjoy working with the community in which they have grown up. Hemalkasa is embedded deep in their hearts and minds.

Digant's elder son, Arnav, too, has begun to understand and appreciate his surroundings. He has read about his great-grandfather and grandfather in textbooks. There is still time before the teenager can take a call on his career. But the future merges with the past whenever Dr Prakash Amte sits on the concrete platform under the neem tree in front of his house.

It is here that he—on rare occasions—attends to patients. As he gently sets a broken bone and puts it in a plaster, his four grandchildren watch on with awe. They then run into the house, shouting in unison that they, too, want to become doctors when they grow up.

Matin Bhosale

THE 'LAWBREAKER' SAVIOUR OF HUNDREDS OF CHILDREN

Our next story is from the penumbral region of Vidarbha, where the darkness of centuries is meeting the new light of hope in twenty-first-century India. The story of Matin Bhosale, who is fighting for the future of children from one of the most severely marginalized communities in the country, moves between the shadow lines of morality and hunger. It also hovers along the margins of law. The story begins in the 1980s, on the day Matin's father was looking for an animal or bird to kill to feed his four children, who had not eaten for three days. The genesis of the story, however, goes back to a colonial-era law that branded millions of people criminals at birth.

The British reasoning for the Criminal Tribes Act, 1871, was described thus by jurist James Fitzjames Stephen: '… [P]eople from time immemorial have been pursuing the caste system defined job positions: weaving, carpentry and such were hereditary jobs.

So there must have been hereditary criminals also who pursued their forefathers' profession.'[3]

The law, in one fell swoop, branded millions of people and their unborn children as criminals to be surveilled, restricted and shunned. Independent India had done away with the law in 1952, but the shadow of hundreds of years of marginalization still hangs over the de-notified tribes, as they are now called, as if their fate is entwined inextricably with the dire prediction made for them hundreds of years ago by white colonizers.[4]

So by the time Shankar Nath Bhosale was stalking animals to hunt to feed his four children, moving through the bushes like only hunter-gatherers can, he was not a born criminal in the eyes of the law per se, but his circumstances forced him to live on the fringes of society. The Phanse Pardhi tribe that Shankar Nath belonged to is a de-notified tribe. As a cursory internet search for 'Pardhi gang' would show, newspaper coverage of crimes committed by members of such tribes still brands criminal gangs as being part of the community. Harassment and stigmatization are still part and parcel of the lives of Phanse Pardhis—as documented by numerous

---

3 Nilisha P. Desai and Uday Gaikwad, 'Ethno-Historical Identity Issue of De-notified Tribe in Kolhapur', Conference: Inter-Disciplinary National Seminar on 'Tribal Society: Literature, Culture and Psychographic Relationship', January 2014, https://www.researchgate.net/publication/261107765_Ethno-historical_Identity_Issue_of_De-notified_Tribe_in_Kolhapur

4 Sudharak Olwe, 'Decades After Denotification, Pardhi Tribe Struggles to Shrug Off "Criminal" Tag', The Wire, https://thewire.in/society/decades-after-denotification-pardhis-in-maharashtra-struggle-to-stave-off-criminal-tag

media reports and studies from institutions such as the Tata Institute of Social Sciences.[5]

There are over 2,00,000 Phanse Pardhis in Maharashtra. Phanse Pardhi women and children eke out a miserable living by begging, with a majority of the community living on footpaths or in the open lands on the peripheries of villages and cities.[6] Little children who press their faces against windows of sleek sedans at traffic signals across Maharashtra, one of India's most prosperous states, are often orphans from this tribe. The men mostly work as daily-wage labourers, while many of the older children are ragpickers.[7]

Shankar Nath, a farm labourer, had not received the promised rice in return for work he had done. His wife, who begged for a living, had had no luck. Their four sons had gone without food for three days. A desperate Shankar Nath was trying to catch a rabbit, partridge or quail in the bushes, but he was drawing

---

5 Paankhi Agrawal and Mayank Sinha, 'A report on the Status of Pardhis in Mumbai City', Centre for Criminology and Justice School of Social Work, Tata Institute of Social Sciences, http://castemumbai.tiss.edu/wp-content/uploads/2015/04/Pardhis-In-Mumbai.pdf

6 Sudharak Olwe, 'Decades After Denotification, Pardhi Tribe Struggles to Shrug Off "Criminal" Tag', The Wire, https://thewire.in/society/decades-after-denotification-pardhis-in-maharashtra-struggle-to-stave-off-criminal-tag

7 Prateek Sharma, 'Persecuted for being a Pardhi: Members of this denotified tribe battle bias, daily harassment', Firstpost, 19 March 2018, https://www.firstpost.com/india/persecuted-for-being-pardhi-members-of-this-denotified-tribe-battle-bias-daily-harassment-4396287.html

a blank. Walking home to his hut in Mangroor Chavala village, 30 kilometres from Amravati, a city in the Vidarbha region of Maharashtra, Shankar Nath happened to pass a farm filled with ripe stems of jowar, a kind of millet, loaded with tiny green grains. He plucked a couple of stems. The thought of his family on the verge of starvation was enough to overcome any fear of consequence.

When he reached the settlement where around fifty Phanse Pardhi families had set up their huts made from leaves of the palash tree, Shankar Nath handed over the jowar stems to his wife, who shaved off the grains to prepare hurada, a local dish. After the frugal meal, the family retired for the night. A few hours later, the police arrived and began pulling out the men from the huts.

Shankar Nath was rounded up, along with many others from his village. The charge was that they had stolen 500 kilograms of millet from the farm. There was no question of any protest by these poor people of a nomadic tribe. The men were taken away. A day later, when Shankar Nath's mother and wife went around asking where he had been taken, a policeman told them that he had been put in prison and would be released in four or five days. Shankar Nath, however, stayed in jail for the next three months.

Shankar Nath's second son, Matin, was then five years old. The incident scared the little boy. Unlike his brothers and other members of his community, Matin could not hunt yet. His fear was that with his father in jail, his uncles who were taking care of the family would abandon him and leave him to starve. The Phanse Pardhis hunt using rope—'*phanse*' means noose—but little Matin didn't yet know how to make a noose or use one to catch small animals or birds. So he tried what he knew. He could mimic the call of birds such as quails and partridges. He tried to lure them with these calls. One day, after a couple of attempts, he managed to catch a quail. Thrilled, he rushed to his uncles. 'I caught a bird today. Now I can also come along with you and hunt,' he told them.

While Matin was developing his survival skills, his father was serving time in jail. The others who had been rounded up with him had been released, but Shankar Nath was sentenced to a three-month term—for a crime that Matin believes his father did not commit. However, those three months in jail were epiphanic for Shankar Nath. As he brooded over his plight and what his family must be facing, one of Shankar Nath's jail mates gave him a life lesson. 'Only education can improve the lot of your family,' the inmate said. 'You have been branded as thieves, so this is what you will get. If you want your children's lives to be better than yours, make sure they study.'

When Shankar Nath walked out of jail after serving his term, he carried with him a new resolve to ensure that his children got a better deal in life. Before poverty could pulverize his determination, Shankar Nath took his four sons to the village school and pleaded with the headmaster to admit them. Either due to his zeal to see his children educated or sheer luck, the headmaster agreed to take them in. Matin was admitted to Class I.

The new routine of going to school and sitting in class was cumbersome for the unbridled spirit of Shankar Nath's sons. The prejudice of their classmates did not help. Even the teacher in Matin's class warned the other children, 'All of you keep your belongings safe—a Phanse Pardhi boy is in the class now.' The students would call Matin a thief and 'Pardhi', using the name of his community as a slur. His siblings also got the same treatment. The constant insults made Matin and his brothers stop going to school. Their absence did not go unnoticed. The headmaster called Shankar Nath to the school and declared, 'Your children are not attending school. You people do not want to change. Take your children out from the school.'

Shankar Nath begged the principal to give them one more chance. The headmaster relented but the brothers refused to return to school. 'We will not go back—everybody, including the teacher, calls us thieves,' they told their father. After much persuasion, only Matin agreed to go back to school.

By now, Shankar Nath knew that merely sending Matin to school was not enough. The father began to visit the school and wait outside the principal's office and staff room until classes got over. Then he would gift his child's teachers crudely packed honey that he had freshly drawn from a hive, or medicinal herbs and plants, and, occasionally, a partridge or quail he had hunted. Gradually, two of the teachers were won over. Matin reached Class IV more for the leniency of his teachers than for his scholastic abilities.

More than the modest gifts his father brought for the school staff, what worked for Matin was the benevolence of Vijay Sardar, the class teacher of Class V. Sardar showed unexpected kindness towards Matin. He bought the boy a school uniform set, a school bag, a slate, books and stationery. Not used to being cared for, Matin did not know how to reciprocate. So he showed his gratitude in the only way that was possible for him—by being a diligent student.

As he began to study, words struck chords in his heart. He was most moved by the poems, prayers and songs that he read and heard in school. '*Le mashal chal pade hai log mere gaon ke/Ab andhera jeet lengey log mere gaon ke* [People of my village have now set out with a torch/They will vanquish the darkness with the light of their knowledge],' was one such song by poet-politician Balli Singh Cheema that shone like a beacon of hope for him.

The lyrics spoke of what human beings could be, what the world should be. He began to draw inspiration from them. The life stories of personalities such as Mahatma Gandhi, Dr B.R. Ambedkar and Chhatrapati Shivaji Maharaj also left a deep impression on his young mind. They ignited his spirit and inspired him to dream of being the change.

The reality of being a Phanse Pardhi, however, dawned once again on Matin Bhosale when he was sixteen years old. One day, when he went to a ration shop to buy subsidized food grains, the shopkeeper told him, 'To buy grains from here you will need a ration card.' The Class IX student was perplexed—he did not even know what a ration card was, let alone have one. When he asked around about how to get one, he was told that he needed a caste certificate to get a ration card for his family. So he asked where he could get a caste certificate from. When he did figure out the government office to go to, the official told him, 'Get your identification papers and address proofs if you want a caste certificate.' This was an astonishing discovery for Matin. Being nomads, most Phanse Pardhis didn't have any kind of identification paper.

Matin understood how important a caste certificate was. He explained the situation to the people of his community, who were as surprised as he was at the concept of identification papers. Fifty of them decided to help him get them their caste certificates. In 2001, the Phanse Pardhi community in Amravati hit the roads and disrupted traffic to draw attention to their demand for caste certificates. It took a month for the district administration to take cognisance of the agitation and the significance of their demand. It took another six months for the government to order officials to survey all settlements of the Pardhi tribe in and around Amravati. The officials identified 1,200 families and issued caste certificates to them.

Matin, meanwhile, was training to join the paramilitary after clearing his Class X board exams with flying colours, in no small measure aided by the confidence boost of leading a successful agitation. That year, the Central Reserve Police Force (CRPF) held a recruitment camp at Hingna near Nagpur, around 150 kilometres from Mangroor Chavala. Matin decided to give it a try. It was easy for the well-built boy to clear the physical test. He was selected and began his training in the CRPF. Twenty days into the training, shooting practice started. Matin could not wield the gun properly and the butt rammed his shoulder on recoil. The injury was pretty bad. Unable to continue with the training routine, on the pretext of going to the bathroom, Matin escaped from the camp.

He returned home to hostility and disappointed looks from his family. His failure to settle down in a government job—as good as it could ever get for a Phanse Pardhi boy—came as a shock to them. The next morning, when the people in the Pardhi settlement discovered that he had run away from the training camp, they ridiculed him. 'What a coward you are to give up just after twenty-one days,' his relatives taunted him. Others said, 'Now you will be back to begging on the streets.'

Shankar Nath, however, was sympathetic. When a CRPF constable came to inquire why Matin had quit, Shankar valiantly told him, 'It would be better if he begs for a living. My son cannot take so much physical stress.' The irony was not lost on the constable. Before leaving, he told Matin, 'So you will go back to begging? And who will give alms to a tall and tough guy like you?'

These words shook Matin. A job in the CRPF would have improved the life of his entire family. He knew that without the job, he would again have to go back to begging, stealing and hunting. He could see only one way out of this vicious circle his community was stuck in—education. Matin took admission in Class XI and cleared his Class XII board exams in 2004. The same year, as he turned twenty, Matin married Seema, the Class VI-pass daughter of his maternal uncle.

Stung by the ridicule of his community for not joining the CRPF, Matin vowed to show them that there were other ways to ensure a better tomorrow for not just his family but for his entire tribe. He decided to regroup the volunteers of the agitation for caste certificates and floated the Adivasi Phanse Pardhi Sudhar Samiti, or Phanse Pardhi reform society. Soon, he learnt that camps were held by Scheduled Caste/Scheduled Tribe organizations to educate communities about their rights and government facilities for them. Matin travelled throughout the Marathwada region to attend these camps, and learnt about the rights and benefits his community, too, was entitled to.

In 2005, an advertisement appeared in a local newspaper for the post of a teacher in a district school in Melghat. The post was only for nomadic tribe candidates. Matin applied for it and got the job in a school in Ghatan, near Dharni, around 100 kilometres from Mangroor Chavala. His family and tribe were ecstatic. For the first time, someone from among them was going to become a teacher.

The newly appointed teacher arrived in Ghatan in 2006 along with his wife, and daughter Anjali. He was to teach geography and maths to students from Class I to Class VI. For the first time, Matin experienced the comfort and convenience of having a regular income and a permanent job. He knew that it was all because of the kindness of his teachers and the education he had received. He looked at his job as a way of giving back, of helping other underprivileged children. He also decided to study further, and by 2009 completed a diploma course in education.

In 2007, when the government launched a polio-eradication drive across Maharashtra, a medical team arrived in Mangroor Chavala to administer the vaccine to Pardhi children. A rumour started floating in the community that the medicine was meant to wipe out the tribe. Scared and ill-informed, many parents refused to allow their children to take the drops of medicine. 'We will not allow you to do this. This is a ploy to kill us,' they told the health officers. The media played up the news.

Disturbed by the development, the CEO of the Amravati zilla parishad asked his staff to find a teacher in the district who belonged to the Pardhi community, and to transfer him there so that he could convince the villagers to let their children get the vaccine. Matin Bhosale, who hailed from this village and was a Phanse Pardhi, was posted at the zilla parishad school in Ghatan, the CEO was informed. He ordered Matin's transfer to the school in Mangroor Chavala.

Back in his village and among his people, Matin began to explain to them the advantages of getting the children vaccinated. 'This medicine is being given to every child across the country, rich and poor. You also have to do it, or this deadly disease will never be eradicated,' he explained to his illiterate community. He also started motivating the children to study. He managed to get about fifty children enrolled in school. 'Most of them are postgraduates and are working in various jobs now,' says the proud teacher.

Though he was making strides in his life, Matin Bhosale did not forget the miseries and sufferings other members of his tribe faced. Life, too, was carving out a path for him beyond plain pedagogy. He kept hearing of the atrocities that Phanse Pardhis faced at the hands of the police and other people. This disturbed him greatly. A recurring question gnawed at him: How could he improve the lot of his people?

One morning in 2009, as he was taking class, a phone call from a farmer in the adjacent village changed the course of Matin's life. 'The bodies of two boys have been found near a stream close to my farm,' the caller told him. 'I think they are of children from your tribe.'

A fortnight earlier, police had picked up a Pardhi couple for a robbery and arson incident in a village in the nearby district of Yavatmal. The husband and wife were taken away in a highway patrol van early in the morning while they were heading into the bushes to hunt. The couple had two sons, who, after the arrest of their parents, were staying with their uncles. The boys had gone to catch fish and crabs with the elders, and had gone missing.

Matin immediately left for the location. On arrival, his fears were confirmed. Lying on the sides of the stream, their bodies covered with mud and slush, were the two sons of the couple who had been arrested. The boys had slipped and drowned. Garbage was stuck on their faces and in their hair. As Matin bent down to pick them up, their limbs and flesh began to fall apart. The bodies had bloated and rotted.

Martin was crazed with grief and anguish. He could feel the blood being squeezed out of his heart and the air sucked out of his lungs. Something within him snapped as he picked up what remained of the boys—one eight and the other ten years old.

Matin Bhosale was no stranger to the unbearable tragedy of being marginalized, but this incident was not something he could reconcile himself to. As he went through the motions of giving the boys a burial, a resolve began to take shape in his mind.

'My teaching job benefits only me and my family. My community is still suffering and I have to do something,' he decided. Soon after that incident, Matin applied for a three-month leave without pay from the school. He asked the volunteers of his organization to head to different districts and survey Pardhi settlements. Once the settlements were identified, Matin travelled to places such as Nagpur, Washim, Akola, Dhule, Yavatmal, Jalgaon and Mumbai.

He visited railway stations and scouted around traffic signals to locate Pardhi children. He found many of them begging. Most were orphans, or their parents were in jail. The unkempt, half-naked children would beg all day and hand over the earnings to their guardians. The money they got was split between the guardian and the local goon. The children's lives were hell. They never got enough food or clothing. Thrashings and insults were routine, as were substance and sexual abuse.

Matin began to ask such children to come with him to his village. 'I promise I will provide you food, shelter and education,' he told them. Most of them refused and their guardians also violently opposed the suggestion. Born on footpaths and brought up in abject poverty, the children had never known a decent home, forget school. Hardened by life, they were insensitive to Matin's pleas and reasoning.

Not one to give up, he continued to persuade them. Yogita, a girl in Mumbai's busy Dadar station, bluntly told him, 'I will come with you if you give me tobacco and booze.' She was just about eleven years old. It was the same story with most of the other children. Their parents were either dead, behind bars or ailing. When hunger pangs struck, chewing tobacco or drinking liquor was easier and cheaper than getting food most of the time.

Matin did not let the children's insolence trouble or discourage him. He thought about these demands and decided that he would try to fulfil them and wait until the children realized the error of their ways. He was hell-bent on changing their destinies, and ready to bend any rule that came in the way. His lived experience as a Phanse Pardhi, his nomadic upbringing and the constant game of hide-and-seek that his tribe played with the cops had instilled a spirit of recklessness in Matin Bhosale. In his desperation to do good, he, over the years, has come to sometimes not consider the right or wrong of the means to that end.

'In my younger days,' Matin says, 'when I was trying to gather people from my community for getting their identification documents, I would often think about Gandhi and how he mobilized and motivated such a large number of people to work with him. I admired Gandhi for his teachings of non-violence and satyagraha. He spoke about the importance of the cottage industry to economically empower people, and I understand how this can help the people of my community. I was very impressed by his beliefs, which advocated self-sustenance through farming. I have visited the Nai Taleem school set up by Gandhiji in Wardha and imbibed a lot of good things that are taught there. But as my struggles continued and I faced problem after problem, I realized that this country has forgotten Gandhi and his values. Somewhere, I also realized that I will not be able to achieve anything by taking the Gandhian path. As I attended awareness camps being conducted for Scheduled Caste and Scheduled Tribe individuals, I realized that Dr Ambedkar had laid out a much better path for people like us, and through it we could fight for our rights and get all that we were entitled to under the Constitution.'

Through 2011, Matin Bhosale continued his travels to find Pardhi children to rescue, and could finally gather 188 of them from different places. Travelling with the children he managed to convince, Matin was a strange sight—one that aroused suspicion not just among fellow travellers but the law keepers too. That he and the children travelled ticketless did not bother him as he could not afford to buy tickets for all of them. He was beaten up many times on the way and often thrown off the trains along with his brood. He, however, brought them to his village with the promise that through education he would change their lives for the better. He decided he would build a school only for children of his tribe. Towards this purpose, Matin resigned from his job as a schoolteacher in September 2012.

~

Matin's uncle Shankuli Bhosale owned three acres of land in their village. Shankuli used to hunt monitor lizards, pheasants, rabbits and wild boar, and sell them in the markets of Amravati. He had saved some money and used it to buy the land in 1971 for Rs 200. In 2012, on a half-acre piece, Matin built a thatched-roof hut with his savings as a teacher and the money made from selling the six goats his family owned. He was setting up a school. He enrolled the children he had gathered from different places in this school. But that was not enough. Soon, realization dawned that though he had spent all that he had to set up this school, it was a mere speck in front of the enormity of the task he had undertaken. The best of his intentions were losing out to more practical and pressing problems. Like hunger.

The school and the children's education took a back seat as the struggle to feed so many mouths began. Matin moved around his community and in the city of Amravati, pleading with people to give him rice and dal so he could feed these children. 'I had acted hastily without thinking the details through,' recalls Matin, who had to struggle every day just to find food for the children he had gathered. 'For nearly one-and-a-half years, the only meal that I could provide them was a gruel made by boiling rice in plenty of water and salt.'

Around August 2013, Matin decided that instead of begging for food, it would be better if he tried to raise funds for his school. Once again, he adopted the only fundraising activity that he knew of—begging. He started a 'Bheek Mango Andolan', or begging revolution, to raise money for the school building. 'I first asked my entire community to pay me a rupee each towards the cause, and then I approached different organizations for funds,' explains Matin. The Magsaysay award-winner Dr Prakash Amte helped him a lot. 'He sympathized with my cause and gave me money for it,' Matin remembers. 'After this, many other organizations and individuals came forward to help.'

From rations, clothes and stationery items to monetary donations, he received aid from all kinds of organizations and individuals, including media houses, lawyers and other professionals. In three years, he raised about 4 crore. Matin began building his school in 2014. He dug two wells and constructed four concrete and three mud-walled classrooms on the land adjacent to where the wells had been dug. A playground, a library, toilets, an open-air stage and concrete slabs for children to sit and study on were set up. On the half-acre land that belonged to his uncle, now registered in the name of the Adivasi Phanse Pardhi Samiti, a two storey concrete hostel was built. Boys and girls from places such as Amravati, Beed, Dhule, Washim and Yavatmal stayed and studied in the school.

'Many of these children had suffered such neglect that they had not had a bath in months. We had to introduce them to the basics of good hygiene,' says Matin about the early days.

His mind, however, was plagued by uncertainty. Anxieties about the future of his community and the apprehensions of whether the school would get recognition from the government—or even be allowed to continue—loomed large, like a humongous question mark. Thus, Matin named his school Prashnachinha Adivasi Ashramshala, which translates to 'Question Mark Tribal Residential School'.

Gradually, thanks to the donations coming in, he equipped the classrooms with blackboards and furniture. Voluntary organizations provided books for the library. By 2018, his school strength had increased to 447 students. Matin's three children were also enrolled there. His wife, Seema, took care of the hostel and the kitchen. As he had promised, the education offered was free of cost. When the number of students in his school increased, Matin appointed eight teachers, four of them from his community. He used a portion of the three-acre land to grow vegetables. Two-hundred fruit trees were also planted, so that the children could savour the taste of mango, sapota, Indian blackberry and guava.

Matin had already applied for affiliation with the education department in 2011, pleading that Phanse Pardhi students required a separate school because of the discrimination they faced. 'But the administration did not grant permission and asked me to enrol the children in the government school,' he says. 'Permission was given only to run a hostel.' Hence, the Class X students from his school now fill their forms for the board exams from the school in Melghat where Matin had once been a teacher.

With sheer hard work and grit, Matin created an oasis for the orphans of his community, children of a lesser God hungry for love, care and kindness. The classrooms began to throb with the sounds of young kids learning maths tables, poems and songs. The playground bustled with the cries and cheers of young boys and girls, as teams locked with each other for kabaddi and kho-kho matches.

The steady donations also ensured that he could pay salaries to the staff of teachers and helpers appointed in the school. The children who were once addicted to alcohol and chewing tobacco were now sitting in the classrooms, poring over textbooks and notebooks. Over the next couple of years, fifty of Matin's students cleared the Class X board exams. The girls' kabaddi team won taluka- and state-level competitions in 2017 and 2018.

Unfortunately, this temple of education so painstakingly built by Matin had shaky foundations. In his desperation to do something concrete for the deprived and poverty-stricken children of his tribe, he had broken some rules. The three acres of land on which the school had been built actually belonged to the government. Matin had encroached upon it. He had no claim over it.

In 2013, he tried to legalize his action by writing letters to the administration, asking them to give him the title of the land as he was using it for the purpose of education, but that did not happen. Two years later, he heard about the possibility of a highway coming up where his school stood. The rumour turned true when the very next year, government officials surveyed the area.

The state government had planned a 700-kilometre Samruddhi Highway, literally prosperity highway, that would connect Nagpur at the centre of India with Mumbai on the west coast. From the time he first heard about it until the government initiated action, Matin made all possible efforts to meet politicians and bureaucrats, and ask them to hand over the ownership of the encroached land. But in vain.

On a hot morning in the first week of June 2019, the children of Prashnachinha Adivasi Ashramshala heard low rumbling sounds. The school was closed for summer vacation, but a handful of students, who had nowhere to go, were staying in the hostel along with the staff and Matin's family. When they saw the big machine take a turn from the road and enter through the gates of their school, they saw their worst fears staring them in the face. As the truth of the moment dawned upon them, they began to scream, 'Bulldozer! Bulldozer!'

The mechanized beast rolled across the playground, throwing up mud and dirt, heading towards the structures where the classrooms were located. Initially dumbfounded by the shock of seeing a bulldozer actually arrive on their campus, the staff quickly swung into action, and took out the benches and green writing boards. About 2,000 books were removed from the library.

In a matter of minutes, the machine razed to the ground the concrete and mud-walled classrooms, library, toilets and the kitchen area. One after the other the walls of the classrooms crumbled, which had just the other day throbbed with the sounds of students learning. The bulldozer also dug up the playground and destroyed the trees Matin had planted some six years back. The two-storey concrete hostel with ten rooms, home to seventy girls and sixty-five boys, which was built on the half acre actually owned by the Adivasi Phanse Pardhi Samiti, was the only structure that was not demolished.

For Matin Bhosale, an unending nightmare unfolded. The school was to reopen in two weeks' time. He had no classroom for the 447 children who were looking forward to returning to their idyll of learning. How would meals for the school be prepared now that the kitchen had been pulled down? Where would the children go with the toilets destroyed?

When the school reopened on 26 June, Matin had to shift the classrooms into the hostel premises. The children had to live, eat and study there. When construction began for the highway, the two wells dug by Matin became unusable with dust, debris and waste filling them up. He had to hire water tankers and pay a hefty amount to get water for the school. The playground, which used to be filled with shouts of 'kabaddi kabaddi' and 'kho-kho', now looked like a post-apocalyptic wasteland.

Matin was running from pillar to post trying to garner some support for rehabilitation. Though the school was on encroached land, the district administration took a sympathetic view because of the cause of the children's education. Since the school housed mostly poor, orphaned children, the administration pitched in by arranging funds under corporate social responsibility schemes. The company that was building the highway was nudged into giving Matin Rs 51 lakh. It was a small amount compared to what Matin had initially put in, but the gesture meant that all hope was not lost.

The struggle for rebuilding the school continues to this day.

~

Matin Bhosale's life, the way he tells it, is straight out of noir cinema, complete with stories of run-ins with the law. However, what has remained firm through all the struggles and hardships he has seen is his resolve to improve the condition of his community. He doesn't want any Phanse Pardhi child to beg, steal or die in filthy streams. He has never once regretted his decision of quitting his job as a schoolteacher.

'It was education that gave me this sense to do something for my community,' he says. 'My father had the good sense to put me in a school. It was the kindness shown by my teachers and the good things they taught me that changed my life.'

The partial demolition of his school has not dampened this spirit. Matin is hopeful that he will be able to rebuild it, but this time he will keep the administration on his side and do everything by the book. He is not willing to consider the option of enrolling his students in state-run schools.

'I have picked up these children from footpaths and railway platforms. The purpose behind setting up Prashnachinha was to give these homeless orphans a healthy environment that nurtures them and gives them a chance to build their lives the right way,' he says, steely determination in his voice. To him, it is important that these children live with him under his care. He is convinced that if he sends them away, they will not just drop out of schools but will be back on the streets, once again begging, stealing and getting beaten up.

The poems, prayers and motivational songs that have inspired him through the worst situations still fuel his fight for his community. Every evening in the hostel, he sits with the students and tells them stories of the greats among men, their struggles and how they fought to overcome the obstacles. The children are taught to dream, to rise above the squalor of their existence. A couple of boys take out the harmonium and tabla. Collectively, they sing, '*Deh mandir, chitta mandir ek theyte pararthana/Satya sundar mangalachi nitya ho aradhana* [I pray that may the body and mind be a temple and I also pray that every day may be auspicious, full of truth and beautiful].'

Satish and Shubhada

ENSURING EQUALITY AND EMPOWERMENT

'Take the village people and slum-dwellers in your hands and give them the benefit of your knowledge, skill, insight, constructive work and patriotic spirit. Give the people this true education through the example of your own lives. Let all your activities be directed to the welfare of the people.'

—Mahatma Gandhi[8]

In the late 1990s, bank officials transferred to Gadchiroli district of Maharashtra for the first time would often be surprised to see the number of tribal women coming to the branches. Dressed in their traditional attire and jewellery, they would stand out at the bank counters, filling out forms and waiting to withdraw or deposit money. The high participation of women in something so

8 Divya Joshi, *Gandhiji on Villages* (Mumbai: Gandhi Book Centre, 2002), https://www.mkgandhi.org/ebks/Gandhionvillages.pdf

inextricably linked to independence as banking stood out in this rural, primarily tribal area.

Gadchiroli has a large number of self-help groups, which are mostly led by women. By the mid-1990s, two women per self-help group in this remote district had opened their own bank accounts—largely because of the efforts of a couple who have dedicated their lives to the rural-development clarion call of Mahatma Gandhi via his apostle Jayaprakash Narayan and ideological heir Vinoba Bhave.

For three decades, Dr Satish Gogulwar and Shubhada Deshmukh have brought healthcare and empowerment to Kurkheda and its neighbouring villages, about 150 kilometres from Nagpur. 'Doctor Saab' and 'Tai' (elder sister), as they are known to the villagers, arrived in Kurkheda in 1984 with their one-year-old son, Sushant. Since then, they have worked for the people towards the vision of self-sufficient villages—from helping combat infant mortality and reviving the traditional system of tribal medicine, to helping win rights over forest produce and a successful campaign for prohibition. And in many other ways.

'We were inspired by the dreams of Gandhi for the villages,' says Satish. 'Bapu had said that people in the villages should be empowered enough to know their rights and obtain them. By helping these people claim their forest rights and get a stake in forest produce such as mahua, tendu and different varieties of vegetables that grow organically in forests, we have been able to move towards Gandhi's vision and goals.'

The self-help groups that Satish and Shubhada set up three decades ago are still thriving. The Amhi Amchya Arogyasathi—loosely 'we for our health'—that the couple run has expanded manifold in scope and size. That a steady stream of students from many schools of social sciences and volunteers come and study.

The story of how the two followed their ideological dream is the story of their labour of love. And in their story, the woman has always had equal rights.

It begins in a public garden in Nagpur in 1981, when the young Satish Gogulwar, a freshly minted MBBS degree holder, was to meet Shubhada Deshmukh, who was doing her master's in social work. He wanted a wife who would share his vision for the future. She wanted to marry on her terms. What they had in common was the romance of the revolution.

~

Satish Gogulwar, from Chandrapur, had arrived in Nagpur to study medicine in 1975, a tumultuous year when India witnessed not only the Emergency imposed by the then Prime Minister Indira Gandhi but also the peak of the Sampoorna Kranti, or Total Revolution, spearheaded by Jayaprakash Narayan. It was the most significant political movement since Independence, one that would shape India's future, grooming a new crop of leaders and a generation that believed in giving back to society.

In JP, as that generation of idealistic Indians called Jayaprakash Narayan, the young Satish Gogulwar found a leader he could follow. In school Satish was influenced by books on Gandhi and Vinoba Bhave. Now in his youth, JP's philosophy and speeches inspired him. When the Emergency ended twenty-one months after it was declared, the elections threw up a new government in New Delhi, and JP formed a national youth organization, the Chhatra Yuva Sangharsh Vahini, of which Satish became an active member even while studying medicine. During his vacations, he travelled to rural areas in Uttar Pradesh, Bihar and Rajasthan to understand the sufferings and hardships of the real India that lived in villages. Even before he started his MBBS course, he had made it clear to his father that he would be working in rural areas, just as Dr Prakash Amte did.

Baba Amte, Dr Prakash's Amte's father, who had set up the Lok Biradari Prakalp in Gadchiroli's Hemalkasa, was a source of inspiration for many young and idealistic men and women of the time, especially in the Vidarbha region. Satish had attended a *shram sanskar shibir*—a service camp—organized by Baba Amte in Somnath village in Chandrapur. Baba Amte's work for the leprosy afflicted had inspired Satish to dream of serving the poor.

This desire to serve the needy in the rural areas came as a shock to the well-off Gogulwar family. His father hoped five years of medical college would drill some sense into his scholarly, idealistic son.

Satish was twenty-seven years old when he completed his medical education. JP had instructed that Vahini members had to quit the organization on turning thirty and serve in the villages. Fortunately for Satish, his seniors Dr Abhay Bang, Dr Ulhas Jaju and Dr Anand Phadke had set up an initiative called Medical Friend Circle in Wardha. Their work was on community health and they deliberated upon policies. Dr Bang had also formed the Chetna Vikas Sanstha in Wardha, which was attached to the district hospital. The organization's work was not limited to administering medical treatment—it involved creating health and medical awareness in the remotest corners of the district. To achieve this, Dr Bang had trained the village women as healthcare workers.

The young Dr Gogulwar approached Dr Bang for an internship and did community work through the sanstha for one-and-a-half years. When Dr Bang and his wife, Dr Rani Bang, decided to go abroad to do their master's degree, they advised Satish to do his post-graduation as well. He, however, decided to return to the villages. 'The villages don't even have simple MBBS doctors. My presence there would bring some relief,' he told them. Satish decided to join his childhood friend Mohan Hirabai Hiralal, who, at the time, was working in Wadsa Desaiganj in Gadchiroli with socialist tribal leader Sukhadeobabu Uikey.

In Chandrapur, Dr Gogulwar's family members were aghast that he was still looking at life through idealistic lenses. The idea of serving in villages was beyond their comprehension. His father thought that getting rid of this zeal required the good old pill—getting the boy married. He began a frantic search for a bride for his son.

This alarmed Satish, for whom JP's socialist philosophy and principles were sacrosanct. JP had advocated that the youth should marry outside their caste to fight the social scourge of casteism. Satish's father was adamant that his son marry a girl from their own community. For Satish, it was important that his life partner at least agree with JP's philosophy and the way of life he had chosen for himself.

~

Shubhada Deshmukh grew up in a household where progressive vision and conservative thought rubbed shoulders. She inherited her grit from her mother, who lived by the rules set by her husband but also found her own space within the household. Shubhada's mother had joined the Rashtriya Sevika Samiti; her attending RSS meetings was not appreciated by the family but she stood her ground in the face of stiff opposition. Shubhada was radical in her own way—to the Left. She grew up in Wardha with a treasure trove of books her grandfather had collected. She was particularly drawn to the works of Marathi author, teacher, social activist and freedom fighter Pandurang Sadashiv Sane. It was through the writings of Sane Guruji, as he was popularly called, that the idea of serving in villages germinated in Shubhada's mind.

Wardha district was also home to Vinoba Bhave's Paunar Ashram and the influence of his ideology was, in some ways, inevitable. Shubhada's grandfather was a doctor who had shunned his medical practice and taken to farming. Her father took up farming even before he had finished his education. A man of traditional values, Shubhada's father brought up his two daughters in a strict, conservative Brahmin environment.

Away from the watchful eyes of the male members, in the kitchen and places where they cooked and ate together, the women of the extended family spoke of progressive ideas—such as how to fight caste and empower their own gender. A key theme of the conversations was identity and how a woman could establish it. The women of the Deshmukh household were educated and voracious readers. They were aware of what was going on in society and were willing to fight obscure and archaic traditions and customs. These discussions left a strong impression on Shubhada and built her into something of a fighter herself. A litmus test awaited her when she completed her graduation.

Her father decided that it was time for her to get married. By then, Shubhada had become part of the Chhatra Yuva

Sangharsh Vahini in her college. She declared that she wanted an intercaste marriage with no dowry given. She had dropped a bomb on the Brahmin household.

Her mother was convinced that she would elope with someone from another caste. 'Don't worry, I will definitely not marry without informing you or without your consent,' Shubhada told her. However, it was stifling at home and the thought of running away did cross her mind. Her mother and aunts came to her rescue—they decided that she would go to Nagpur to do her post-graduation and live with one of her aunts. Her father expressed his displeasure. 'She is going to study further—there is nothing wrong in it,' her mother argued and, once again, stood her ground. Shubhada did leave home, but father and daughter were not on talking terms for the next six months.

In Nagpur, Shubhada found that her course in social work barely piqued her interest. It was a new discipline, and the faculty had no practical experience. It was difficult to learn about fights for social justice sitting in a classroom. She began to bunk classes to take part in various protests being organized in the city, just to get a feel of real-life scenarios. She also began to study the Rozgar Mazdoor Sanghatan, which had organized female labourers and was encouraging them to save their earnings. She would visit construction sites where these women were employed, and watch how hard they worked, how they faced exploitation and yet seemed content. She observed them as they sat together to eat, admired their spirit as they sang songs while working and tending to their children at the work site. These scenes kindled memories of the discussions back home, when the women in her family would sit together and talk about their rights and the freedom to choose what they wanted to do.

One of Shubhada's teachers, Arun Kumar, was from Bihar and he had been part of JP's Vahini. His lectures gave her a deeper understanding of social movements. She started reading books on Gandhian thought and began to understand why the Mahatma urged the youth to serve in villages. By now, her master's course was coming to an end and the pressure of returning home to get married once again loomed over her. 'It is not marriage that I am trying to avoid,' she told her friends. 'It is more important for me to marry someone who thinks like I do.'

A friend suggested that Shubhada meet Dr Satish Gogulwar. 'He has similar thoughts and ideas about service,' the friend told her. Shubhada's younger sister had met Satish at a camp organized by the vahini. She seconded the idea.

The paths of Satish Gogulwar and Shubhada Deshmukh crossed in a public garden in Nagpur, and it was clear to them that their way forward was together. Be it wanting a simple, intercaste marriage or the wife retaining her maiden name, they were cut from the same ideological cloth—of JP's philosophy. They also realized there would be opposition from both their families and decided they would wait for a year and try to convince their parents. 'It will be good if I utilize this time to travel to places such as Gujarat, Uttar Pradesh, Bihar and Madhya Pradesh to get first-hand knowledge about life in villages,' Shubhada told Satish. 'That way I will stay away from home.'

They got married on 25 December 1982 in a civil ceremony held on the premises of a court in Wardha. Satish's parents did not attend the wedding, nor did they bless the couple. Soon after, the newlyweds left for Wadsa. They had, of course, decided that they would not take anything from their parents.

Shubhada wore her feminism on her sleeve. Not only did she not change her name, she also shunned symbols such as the bindi, mangalsutra and bangles—the marks of a married woman in India. It would have prompted comment in the cities too, and in the village it bordered on blasphemous. The villagers cast doubts on her religion and berated her for not following social norms. In 1984, Shubhada gave birth to a son. He was named Sushant Shubhada Satish, taking the parents' names and no surname.

JP's vision for India, like the Mahatma's, was real grassroots change across the country. Though service was an important component, the stress was on changing mindsets, as that would mean true empowerment. Satish and Shubhada began to focus on this as they settled into their new life. What they found surprised them as well.

In 1978, the Maharashtra state government had launched an Employment Guarantee Scheme. A job seeker had to write an application to the *talathi*, the local revenue official, and the administration would have to provide employment within fifteen days of the application, else the applicant would be entitled to unemployment allowance of Re 1 per day. Satish began to inform the villagers about the scheme and published a simple brochure about what it entailed. The villagers, delighted to know about this programme, went to the local talathi's house to hand over the applications. The talathi claimed there was no such scheme but the villagers refused to budge until they were given the signed receipts for their applications.

Unnerved by the impromptu agitation, the official sent an SOS to the local police station. Soon, a policeman came to check.

'We only want acknowledgement for the forms that we have come to submit,' the villagers told him. The cop instructed the talathi to give each one of them the required receipt. This was a major victory for the villagers. They had discovered the power of satyagraha—the most potent weapon in the armoury of Mohandas Karamchand Gandhi.

Increasing demands for work or unemployment allowance began to irk the talathis, who started allocating jobs to the villagers in far-flung places. However, Satish had told them that according to the scheme, if the job was more than 5 kilometres from their homes, the government had to provide a travel allowance and make arrangements for their stay as well. He had also taught them simple math to help them calculate wages to ensure they were not short-changed.

Gadchiroli district, which shares borders with the states of Chhattisgarh and Telangana, has seen many forms of social mobilization under leaders of tribal communities. When Mohan Hirabai Hiralal, and later Satish, arrived in Wadsa to work for the people, the tribal leader Sukhadeobabu Uikey joined hands with them. Later, when Sukhadeobabu decided to contest elections, Mohan, Satish and others decided it was time to move away.

So far, Satish and Mohan had been working under the banner of a trade union. Funds were coming from friends, through local contributions and other donors. Now they needed to form an organization. But there was unanimity among them that they would not form a single institution, as that often led to conflict. They decided it was time to branch out and pursue a path that was of interest to them.

Satish and Shubhada came to Kurkheda and set up the Amhi Amchya Arogyasathi.

Kurkheda, along with Armori and Korchi, are part of the Desaiganj subdivision of Gadchiroli district. It has a large tribal population. When Satish and Shubhada arrived there in 1984, the Jagruk Adivasi Sanghathan established by Sukhadeobabu was already working for the land rights of tribal people.

~

When Shubhada Deshmukh and Dr Satish Gogulwar arrived in Kurkheda in 1984 with their toddler son, Sushant, all they could afford was an old mud house that was almost falling apart. The couple shifted in with a bed, a few utensils and a stove. There was no toilet, so Satish dug up a pit a distance from their home, which they would use at night. It was not for them to complain. They had chosen this path.

One day, as Shubhada was cooking while her toddler son was lying on the bed, a portion of the roof came crashing down, missing the baby by a whisker. 'It left us shattered and shaking,' says Satish. 'But we learnt to live with our constraints,' Shubhada interjects. 'Like I could not have foreseen that Satish, despite being a doctor, would not be available when I would need him the most.'

She then recalls the time when her son had diarrhoea, which can be life-threatening in remote areas, and Satish was away in another village. 'Fortunately, I was able to locate a doctor in Kurkheda, who administered treatment to Sushant,' she remembers. Household chores were, of course, shared by both. For the villagers, this understanding between the couple was a constant source of shock. 'They would mock me when I went to hang our clothes out for drying or take care of our son when Shubhada went out for meetings,' says Satish, smiling as he remembered those moments. 'Our society continues to be male-dominated and the men in the village would often ask me why my wife couldn't manage the house while I worked. I would often point out to them that their wives, too, went to work in farms along with the men.'

Their son studied in the local school until Class V. After that, he shifted to Nagpur, where he lived with his aunt, Satish's sister.

But soon Shubhada and Satish had to take charge of two little girls.

One day, a teacher from a local school near Kurkheda knocked on their door. He had with him two little girls—one six years old and the other four. 'Their parents have died in a mishap and the relatives are not willing to take the responsibility of these girls,' he told Satish. The younger child was developmentally challenged. 'You are the only two people in whose care I can leave these poor orphans,' the teacher said. Any doubts they had—both Shubhada and Satish had to travel frequently to far-flung areas—vanished the minute they saw the frightened faces of the girls. They decided to look after the sisters until alternative arrangements could be made.

However, despite their best efforts, they could not find a foster home or any relatives willing to adopt the girls. All this while, the little girls grew closer to Satish and Shubhada. When no other arrangement seemed possible, they legally adopted the girls, Bharati and Madhuri.

Bharati, who, like her mother, did her post-graduation in social work, is now married and lives with her husband in Kurkheda. Madhuri lives and works with her parents. She is also married and is a mother. Sushant lives and works in Pune.

Shubhada and Satish were familiar with Gadchiroli, but to assimilate even better, they initiated the concept of community weddings to cut costs for the families. 'This brought many eligible boys, girls and their families from different villages to Kurkheda,' remembers Shubhada. 'Once the matches were fixed, we would ask the villagers to make contributions like rice and other food items for the village feast, and also ask the more prosperous ones to gift a utensil or some such item to the young couples.' The practice continued for fifteen years, but Satish and Shubhada distanced themselves from it once the government began to provide financial help for these events.

Both of them were aware that true change in society could be brought about only when women were treated as equals. To work towards this goal, Shubhada began to hold meetings with the women in Kurkheda and its surrounding villages. They began to discuss demands for gender equality, including equal say in matters concerning the village.

'Once, a woman complained about her abusive husband,' remembers Shubhada. 'We tried to counsel her and the husband, but the situation worsened and a police case had to be filed against the man. This rattled him and he died by suicide. The local MLA began to insinuate that I was responsible for the tragedy, but the women in my group stood by me and defended me.'

~

In the late 1980s and early 1990s, when Dr Satish Gogulwar and Shubhada Deshmukh were settling down in Kurkheda, a slew of social movements were under way in the region. The couple noticed that women were conspicuously absent from these agitations and seldom voiced their opinion. They decided to change that.

They began by gathering women at Kurkheda to form self-help groups (SHGs) An SHG pools resources to make the participants financially stable. The women voluntarily come together to save small sums of money every month. The members are allowed to dip into these collective savings in times of emergency to cope with a paucity of funds, for purchasing assets or for important events in their lives.

By 1986, Dr Abhay and Dr Rani Bang had also started working in this region. They formed an organization called SEARCH to work on child and infant mortality. They trained local women as midwives to assist in childbirth and neonatal care. Satish, Shubhada and the Bangs were all engaging with tribal women. Satish and Shubhada were organizing them to form SHGs while the Bangs were training them to be barefoot doctors. As they learnt about the concerns and lives of these women, one very common and disruptive problem that emerged was alcoholism among the men.

Tribal communities distil their own liquor from mahua—and the indiscriminate drinking among men was ruining families. More than unemployment, alcoholism was the bigger cause of poverty. 'Our sufferings will considerably reduce and the lives of our children will get better if liquor is banned,' the tribal women told the two couples.

Satish and Shubhada, along with the Bangs, launched a movement for banning alcohol in Gadchiroli. It took them seven years to get the government to act, which relented and imposed prohibition in the district in 1992.

Though their initiatives were yielding positive results, money was hard to come by, and Satish and Shubhada were struggling to sustain themselves. With no regular source of income, they were surviving on aid from small organizations and managing with a bit of help from their friends. It was around this time that a project on production of tussar silk brought monetary relief and gave them the required momentum.

For this they had to travel to the neighbouring district of Chandrapur, and the tussle was largely about rights over forests.

From time immemorial, the tribal communities have been surviving on the forests around them and have also been their protectors. They worship trees and perform rituals around them. The forests are a source of livelihood for the tribals and a means of sustenance too, as a large variety of vegetables and agricultural products used extensively in their kitchens, such as mahua, grow organically there.

Since Independence, when a number of government departments and agencies came into force to safeguard the natural wealth of forests, the rules began to alienate the tribals from what was their natural habitat. Their struggle for forest rights began from this time.

The thick, dry deciduous forests of Chandrapur are known for their rich vegetation. The jungles are famous for teak, bamboo, arjuna (*Terminalia arjuna*) and yen (*Terminalia tomentosa*) trees, on which silkworms thrive.

The Dhivar samaj, or the fisherfolk of Vidarbha, produce tussar silk, or wild silk, as it is also known. They obtain the threads from the cocoons of silkworms, which thrive on the arjuna and yen trees. In the 1990s, the Central Silk Board signed a project with the Swiss government to help tribals adopt more scientific methods of collecting tussar threads. Officials of the board approached Satish for help. Hard-pressed for funds, Satish and Shubhada decided to take up the project, even though it involved commuting to the forests in Chandrapur.

Satish was alarmed when he saw that the forest department had taken up a drive to plant teak and bamboo trees in the forest, and was cutting down arjuna and yen trees—probably because teak and bamboo fetched more money. He wrote to the department, pointing out how it would deprive the tribal community of a means of livelihood. When there was no response from the officials, he told the tribals that they would have to launch an agitation.

The tribals wrote a letter to the district forest officer, informing him about the agitation. On the decided day, a thousand tribal men and women entered the forest carrying an arjuna sapling each on their heads, which they would plant in place of the saplings put in by the forest staff. They were stopped by officials, who told them, 'We understand the issue. You will have to end this agitation but we assure you that we will not cut down the trees.' The felling of arjuna and yen trees stopped after that, Satish says.

He and Shubhada also saw how vulnerable the silk collectors were to exploitation by moneylenders. The fishermen often took loans from the local moneylender to tide over a lean period until they got paid for the threads they had sold. The village moneylender levied a hefty interest. If they borrowed Rs 100, they had to repay Rs 150 after six months.

Shubhada and Satish decided to organize the Dhivar women in an SHG. However, the fishermen had no steady income, so there was no question of savings. The National Bank for Agriculture and Rural Development, or NABARD, came to their rescue and provided a loan to the community to help them kick-start their savings for the SHG. This was a boon for the destitute families of the community. They could now take loans from the group and their dependence on the traditional village moneylender decreased.

By 1996, Satish and Shubhada had set up a network of SHGs around Kurkheda, which revolutionized the lives of the women in the area. They were more independent and economically self-reliant. The grateful women acknowledged the role Satish and Shubhada had played in empowering them. It was not just the community they were serving that began to appreciate their work. Recognition came from their own families too.

One day, Satish got a call from his home in Chandrapur. 'I would now like to come and stay with you at Kurkheda,' Satish's father told him. Vasant Gogulwar sold off his property in Chandrapur and gave the money to his son. 'You use this to build a house here,' he said. This helped Satish buy a plot of land in Kurkheda and take a bank loan to build the premises of Amhi Amchya Arogya Sathi. The family still lives and works from the one-acre campus.

It houses the office, guest rooms and volunteer lodgings, apart from the living quarters of Satish and Shubhada, a two-bedroom facility facing a lush garden that leads to a verandah where one can sit and relax. A large collection of books occupies the living room and also offers space to the family to come together when they are all in Kurkheda.

Around the mid-1990s, another government scheme brought Satish and Shubhada closer to the community they served. The CEO of the zilla parishad asked Shubhada to conduct a study of all the existing groups in the district under the Development of Women and Child in Rural Areas, or DWACRA, a microfinance scheme that the Indian government had launched in the early

1980s. Under the scheme, a group of skilled women could get a loan of up to Rs 10,000. However, not everybody knew about it.

Shubhada surveyed all the six subdivisions of the district and found that 80 per cent of the DWACRA groups that had received funds were defunct. When she submitted the report, the CEO ordered his officers to recall the loans. He then entrusted to Amhi Amchya Arogya Sathi the task of forming 100 such groups—a tough task in the Maoist-affected district. Shubhada appointed volunteers to fan out in all the divisions. It was decided that they would first form SHGs, identify the ones that had the potential for running an enterprise and give those SHGs loans. The volunteers set up 1,600 groups in three months.

The success of these SHGs helped Satish and Shubhada encourage the women to open and operate their own bank accounts. The couple chose two women from each SHG and opened an account in each of their names. The group's savings were deposited in these accounts. The women had such faith in their group that nobody hesitated in depositing their savings in the account of their representative.

~

Development in the remote interiors of Chandrapur and Gadchiroli has been slow and the region remains deprived of proper medical services. Hence many quacks thrive here. They are not qualified but they treat patients, even administering antibiotics and other medicines. They are rapidly replacing the traditional tribal healers who use herbs and medicinal plants to prepare traditional medicines.

The tribal healers, who are also shepherds and farmers, are called *vaidu*. Their knowledge about diseases and their cures has been handed down to them by their gurus. The vaidu treats only those ailments of which he has some knowledge. So some treat bone-related problems while others dispense medication for other diseases. They do not charge any money for their medicines or treatment. The practice has continued for generations. 'I discovered them during my forays into far-flung villages, when we were working to set up SHGs,' says Satish.

He began to visit the jungles with the traditional healers to learn about their practices. 'We held profound discussions on medical science; knowledge and ideas were shared freely,' he says. 'Sometimes I was the student learning from them and at others I would be their teacher when I told them about modern medicine and how it was practised.'

As quacks flourished, the vaidu, a storehouse of knowledge about traditional medicine, began to disappear. The younger generation in the tribal community was not willing to learn this skill. A vaidu is obliged to provide treatment free of cost; but the quacks were making quick bucks. This alarmed Satish, who devised a method to preserve and promote this traditional practice. For this, he decided to tap the talent among the women of the SHGs.

In many regions, it is common for the grandmother or an elderly lady of the house to carry a small purse containing spices and herbs to treat simple ailments, such as a stomach ache, headache, nausea, cough and cold. The purse, or potli, is considered the go-to remedy for simple diseases and discomforts. Satish decided that he would seek the help of elderly tribal women to carry forward this skill.

He selected 1,500 women from the SHGs and taught them how to grow five to six medicinal plants each in their backyard.

He travelled across the villages to teach them how. 'I kept the number of women being trained limited as I didn't want to commercialize the process. What was more important was that the traditional skills not disappear,' he says. The initiative led to a revival of interest in traditional tribal medicine.

~

Satish and Shubhada had changed the lives of the community, but the region's biggest curse continued to be child and infant mortality. Back in the 1980s, remote areas and villages were the worst hit as medical facilities were dismal. Dr Bang had started working on this in earnest. To raise a large number of medical volunteers, he began to train village women in neonatal care. They would go into the interiors to spread awareness and provide basic treatments. He wanted this model to be replicated in seven other places across the state. He approached Satish for help, who readily took up the challenge. Between 2001 and 2007, Satish and Shubhada implemented this model of volunteer-training in thirty villages of Korchi taluka of Gadchiroli district.

Septicaemia, diarrhoea and pneumonia were the three big killers, and Satish trained his barefoot paediatricians to identify the symptoms of these diseases and administer the relevant medicines. These women would accompany the midwives, who went to various homes for deliveries, and offer care to the neonates. The crucial practices taught to the volunteers included ensuring that the baby cried after birth, wrapping the baby immediately and helping feed the baby if the mother was unable to do so. Equipped with this training, these women could save infants who were born with birth weights as low as 1.2 kilograms, less than half of what is considered normal. This team moved from village to village, saving the lives of infants who otherwise had slim chances of survival.

Satish recollects one such incident in the early days of this initiative. A young volunteer from his team, who had studied only till Class IV, had gone along with the midwife for a delivery to a village called Allitola. The volunteer, trained in neonatal care, waited outside the hut as the midwife went in to perform the delivery. After a long struggle, a baby girl was delivered, but much to the anxiety of the family and the midwife, she did not cry.

The midwife was clueless, so one of the quacks was called. After struggling for a while, he declared the infant dead. 'Can I take a look at the baby?' the volunteer meekly asked. Out of desperation, the family allowed her. The volunteer immediately bent over the still infant and gave her artificial respiration. After half an hour of hard work, the newborn finally let out a cry that mingled with the shouts of jubilation of the family.

In his chamber in Kurkheda, Satish has a photograph of that girl, clicked seventeen years later. Also in the frame are the volunteer who had saved her, the midwife and the girl's mother. 'Every life saved is a validation of all the hard work undertaken by us and the volunteers,' he says.

~

The example that Satish and Shubhada's Amhi Amchya Arogya Sathi has set ensures that its campus bustles with scores of volunteers—from different schools of social sciences and foundations—who come to Kurkheda to learn from the model created by the couple. The learning process for these new generations of change-makers begins from the moment they arrive here.

The living quarters are spartan single rooms with attached toilets. The resident has to keep the room and toilet clean. Adjacent to the rooms is a kitchen-and-dining area. Locally bought vegetables are placed neatly on the kitchen floor and local women help with the cooking. A gas stove is used to prepare a simple meal—a vegetable, dal, rice and rotis for about fifteen people every day.

The motto is self-help. The food is kept on a stone counter and the young volunteers serve themselves and sit together at the long dining table, where they discuss various projects over the meals. The volunteers carry their plates and glasses, and wash the dishes, wipe them dry and place them back in the dining room. From the washing area, a staircase leads up to a large hall that houses the office of the organization. Pictures of Indian social reformers adorn the walls.

'Serving the less-privileged in remote areas requires immense dedication and sacrifice,' says Satish. 'It is very encouraging to see these young boys and girls come here and adapt to the simple life. Their presence here is crucial, as in the future we will need more youth to come to such places and serve the people.'

Enduring physical hardship, adopting a rural lifestyle and living with meagre financial resources, Satish and Shubhada have succeeded in bringing about real change in the lives of many people. The problems that they had come to tackle three decades ago, however, still remain, and this disturbs them.

'Women still have a very low presence in political decision-making. These are still under the dominance of family and caste factors,' says Shubhada.

'We want more representation of women in gram sabha and panchayats,' says Satish. 'Women should be given equal status in society. Male dominance is part of our mindset and I would say that my wife helped me come out of this by constantly goading me to share work and responsibilities, just as she would share mine. I always say that we have been able to ready many daughters of Savitri bai Phule, but not that many sons of Jyotirao Phule.' Satish is referring to one of the greatest Indian social reformers, educationists and poets from Maharashtra and his wife, who is regarded as the first female teacher of India.

He follows up the reference to the legendary social reformers with a personal one.

'Even my father, who was initially against our marriage and would always complain that Shubhada had retained her maiden name, in the last days of his life, acknowledged that she was an individual in herself and did not require to take up a surname to justify her work or existence.'

Shubhada's biggest fear 'is about the erosion of simple values that govern tribal lives'. 'Every political party today has an extremely individualistic culture,' she explains. 'Tribals, on the other hand, believe in the power of community-living and the process of collective decision-making. My fears are that as development comes, these values will get wiped out.'

When the couple arrived in Kurkheda, the central theme of their work was to promote a culture of self-help and self-governance. With the basic groundwork done, they are concentrating their efforts on making the gram sabha more powerful. In 2015, the two helped set up a federation of ninety gram sabhas in Korchi. They have groomed these local governing bodies on the lines of the one in Mendha Lekha, which works on the principle of governance by consensus.

'Over the next ten or fifteen years, we want them to become self-reliant and take all the required decisions on their own,' says

Satish. 'We want to sustain our work through these institutions of self-governance.'

Satish and Shubhada are still convinced that India needs many more people to dedicate themselves to the task of rural uplift. 'If we have a dream of empowered villages and a strong nation, more educated urban youth will have to come to villages and serve here,' Satish says. 'I see this hope in these young boys and girls who willingly come to Kurkheda as volunteers.'

Ashish and Kavita Satav

HEALING HANDS FOR THE GREATER GOOD

Dr Ashish Satav and his wife, Dr Kavita Satav, woke up one night to the piercing wails of their only son, Athang, who was then a frail, asthmatic three-year-old. The baby was in excruciating pain, but neither parent could pinpoint the cause of the agony. Neither of them was a paediatrician. There was no question of finding another doctor. They were 150 kilometres from a proper hospital, and the way was through deep jungles.

They watched their son suffer, helpless, until Ashish realized that the child had acute pain in his ear. Finding an ENT specialist in Melghat, in Amravati district of Maharashtra, where Ashish and Kavita had settled down to serve the tribal population ravaged by disease and malnutrition, is still difficult—back in 2004 it was next to impossible. Through the night, Ashish kept reading from books on paediatric medicines and treated the boy himself. The pain subsided by morning but Ashish realized Athang must have ruptured a membrane in one ear. He had to be admitted in a hospital in Ashish's hometown Wardha, more than 250 kilometres away.

At the bedside of their child in the city hospital, Ashish and Kavita had to confront their helplessness at not being able to help their son, despite both of them being MD and MS doctors. Of what use was this education when they could not ease the pain of their little boy, they asked themselves. As doctors, they were also aware that the wet and cold climate of Melghat was aggravating their child's asthma.

'It was a vulnerable moment,' Kavita remembers. 'Had we allowed those thoughts to linger for some more time, it would have been impossible for us to return to Melghat.'

Ashish and Kavita Satav did not break. They returned and immersed themselves in their work. Sixteen years later, on 3 January 2020, they would be invited to Rashtrapati Bhavan to meet President Ram Nath Kovind and share their experience of providing healthcare to the tribals of Melghat.

Along the way, Ashish would be conferred a myriad of awards, including the World Health Organization's Public Health Champion Award, REAL Global Award by Save the Children UK, and Best Tribal Research Project Award and Young Scientist Award by the Indian Council of Medical Research.

~

Ashish Satav was thirteen years old when he decided that he would live and work in the villages. It was unusual because of a number of reasons. He was an extremely naughty boy who would often beat up his brothers and get into trouble, for one.

The Satavs are a well-known business family in the district headquarters of Wardha, in Maharashtra's eastern Vidarbha region.

Rambhau, Ashish's father, is a distributor for tractors and two-wheelers, and also owns farmlands. Ashish, the second of Rambhau's three sons, grew up pampered. He was a boisterous child who would often end up with injuries.

When Ashish's maternal grandfather, Vasantrao Bombatkar, a staunch Gandhian, heard about the exploits of his grandson, he decided to channel that energy. Bombatkar had fought for India's Independence along with Mahatma Gandhi, and worked with Vinoba Bhave and Jayaprakash Narayan. He began to introduce Ashish to the lives of these great men. The grandfather gave young Ashish, who was then in Class VII, books on Gandhian thought and told him stories based on the philosophies of Bapu.

It had a transformative effect on the adolescent. *My Experiments with Truth*, which Ashish read when he was thirteen, made an especially deep impact on his mind. Gandhi's observations—that the real India lived in villages and those who wanted to serve the country should go to the villages—resonated with the teenager. He decided that when he grew up, he would live and work in villages.

Bombatkar was moved by the boy's resolve. He, too, had worked to educate and empower farmers in the tribal areas of Nandurbar in Maharashtra. He had seen the misery of those who tilled the land. He knew that serving the poor and the needy was true service to the nation. Ashish's father was also watching closely how his father-in-law was mentoring his son. Rambhau knew Ashish would not swim with the tide, that he would choose a path far from the beaten one.

Ashish did not disappoint his father and grandfather. He would go on to bring healthcare to Melghat, one of India's most backward pockets in one of its most affluent states, and save thousands of lives.

~

Ashish's search to find his *karmabhoomi*, where he would settle down and serve, began in the early days of his studies at the Government Medical College in Nagpur, from where he would complete his MBBS and MD in 1997. During vacations he would not go home to Wardha. Instead, he began visiting the hospitals set up by Dr Prakash Amte and Dr Abhay Bang—both in Gadchiroli district, in the densely forested tribal areas—to serve the poor locals.

Rambhau and his wife, Kamal, suffered from multiple ailments. Ashish was the only doctor in the family, but they made no attempt to prevent him from spending his time in the villages. The medical condition of his parents worried Ashish. The thought of settling down in Gadchiroli, which was closer to Wardha, crossed his mind. This way he could be within reach whenever his parents required medical attention. However, two renowned doctors, Dr Amte and Dr Bang, were already working in that area. Setting up another facility in Gadchiroli would be more about serving his own convenience and less about helping those who needed his attention.

So Dr Ashish Satav zeroed in on Dharni in Melghat, in Amravati district—where tigers roam and malnutrition stalks. Heavy rains lash the region, and for four months in the monsoons it is shrouded in thick cloud and mist.

At the turn of the century, Melghat, about 622 kilometres north-east of Maharashtra's capital of Mumbai, was way beyond the back of beyond. There were hardly any roads and no electricity. Barely two buses plied between Dharni and Amravati, creaking and crawling up the winding ways of the hilly terrain. Dharni, the area Ashish had selected, was at least 100 kilometres from the nearest habitation. With no proper roads, the drive was through thick jungles.

Ashish began to prepare himself for life in that hostile terrain. He stopped using a cooler or a fan even in the harsh summers of Vidarbha, when temperatures soared to 48° Celsius. In the winters, when the mercury plummeted to single digits, he would bathe in cold water.

To build his mental and physical strength, and to help himself remain calm during the adversities that he was sure to face, Ashish began to practise yoga and meditation every day. His vacations were spent in Melghat or Gadchiroli, where he would observe the locals and study their lifestyle. In a way he was now immune to the difficult terrain and inclement weather—the only thing that distressed him was the dismal state of medical aid and the misery of the people living there.

There were only two healthcare centres in the region that Ashish had chosen—one in Dharni, and the other about 85 kilometres away in the hill station of Chikhaldara. Locals had to walk a difficult route through thick forests to reach either of the two. The region saw severe health issues but no facilities for treatment. Ashish vowed to change that.

In 1998, he resigned from the post of lecturer in the department of medicine of the Mahatma Gandhi Institute of Medical Sciences Sevagram and registered a voluntary organization named Mahan. With the money that he had saved during his lectureship and post-graduation, he rented a small four-room house in Dharni that he turned into a hospital, with its outpatient department (OPD) in a mud hut at a nearby village named Kolupur. Dr Ashish Satav, MD, lived in this 'hospital' so he would be available 24x7 to his patients, if and when they came. On the rare occasions they did, he had to do everything himself, including cleaning up their spit and vomit.

He would also frequently visit Dr Ravindra Kolhe—who had made Bairagarh, about 31 kilometres away, his home—to learn about the tribal people and the diseases specific to them. The senior doctor not just mentored him but also became instrumental in finding a life partner for Ashish.

~

The idealistic young physician had certain criteria for the woman who was to be his wife. She had to be a doctor who had graduated from a government medical college, of a different caste and, of course, willing to live in Melghat and serve the poor.

One day, Dr Kolhe's wife, Smita, broke her spectacles and Ashish accompanied her to Amravati to visit an eye specialist, Dr Sandhya Manekar. After the check-up, the group of doctors started chatting. Smita introduced the tall, lean and attractive Ashish to Sandhya, and said they were looking for a suitable match for him but the girl had to be a doctor.

Sandhya was quick in her reply. 'We are also searching for a match for my youngest sister, Kavita, an eye surgeon!'

So Ashish described to Sandhya his work in Melghat and the conditions he had set for his wife-to-be.

'Caste is the biggest cause of disparity and atrocities in society,' he told her, explaining why he wanted to marry a girl from a caste different from his. 'Inter-caste weddings can help weed out this malaise.'

Seeing that Sandhya was interested in his work, Ashish suggested, 'Instead of going to Wardha to meet my parents, why don't you and your family visit Melghat? It would be better if you first saw where and how I live and work.'

Ashish also warned her about the tedious journey to Dharni. 'You will have to spend the night there as there is no return bus the same day,' he told her, and advised that the family carry their own drinking water. He wanted them to harbour no illusions.

When Sandhya informed her parents about the work that Ashish was doing in Melghat, Champatrao and Girija Renge were impressed with the dedication of the young doctor. Champatrao was a forest officer and Girija a schoolteacher. They lived in Akola. Kavita was the youngest of their four children—one boy and three girls—who grew up seeing their parents go out of their way to help others.

Champatrao would often return home without his chappals or shirt, and sometimes even his vest or sweater. When his wife would ask him what happened, he would say he had given it to someone who needed it far more than him. Girija would chide him gently for giving away a sweater that she had so lovingly knitted for him, but would then break into a smile. She, too, felt good about helping those in need.

There was a nursing home close to the residence of the Renges. Girija would send meals for the relatives of patients who would come there from the villages for treatment—even though she did not know them and they hadn't asked her to. It was just something Girija did happily and voluntarily.

Kavita, being the youngest, grew up much loved by all. 'I have always got whatever I wanted,' she says, as her smile lights up her eyes and leaves a glow on her face. The young Kavita hero-worshipped her eldest sister. She was in awe of her sister's aura and the respect that Sandhya would get from her patients. Kavita, determined to follow in her footsteps, got admission for her MBBS at Indira Gandhi Government Medical College in Nagpur in 1993.

In medical college, perhaps thanks to destiny, she got a house job in general surgery. Initially she was reluctant—it was a lot of hard work and a bit scary, she says—but her sister's insistence helped her complete it. That rough-and-tumble experience of the general surgery house job would stand her in good stead in Melghat—in treating patients with different problems and a wide variety of wounds.

Keen on being an ophthalmic surgeon, Kavita was disappointed when she could not get admission in a degree course for post-graduation and just got a diploma seat. A fellow student with fewer marks than her got admission in the degree course. Kavita broke down. Just to humour her, Sandhya said, 'You can go and work in a village and no one will know thc difference or care if you are a degree and a diploma holder.' Kavita, however, had more spunk than to get cowed down by such injustice. She took the matter to court. Before the case could be decided, in her next attempt, she got admission in a degree course. Proud of her success, the family celebrated. Girija bought an entire set of apparatus that an eye surgeon would need.

Being the youngest in the family, Kavita was extremely attached to her parents and siblings. She did a short stint as a lecturer at a medical college in Wardha, but was soon homesick. Staying with her middle sister Chhaaya, who was working there, was a small consolation. Kavita's anxieties for her parents overpowered everything else. She quit her job and returned to Akola. When her brother, an engineer, married an ENT surgeon, Kavita was relieved. Her sister-in-law took charge of the home and the ageing parents.

It was during this time that the family began to look for a match for Kavita.

~

The Renges decided to take up Dr Ashish Satav's offer to visit Melghat. The family packed food, water and set out for a two-day visit to the hilly region. Kavita accompanied them. When they saw the work Ashish was doing, they were impressed as well as conflicted.

After the rounds of the villages, the makeshift hospital and the OPD were over, Kavita's family went into a huddle in the hospital. They liked Ashish's sense of service and the good work he was doing, but they could not imagine their youngest daughter roughing it out in the middle of nowhere.

Long discussions in hushed tones ensued in a room at the hospital, even as Ashish went about his work in the adjacent room. There was near unanimity among the Renges that he should be encouraged. It was also obvious to the family that Ashish could not single-handedly do all that he had pledged to do. A life partner who understood his sentiments and dedication to work for the poor would make his life and work much easier. They felt Kavita could fill that space.

Sandhya, however, took a more practical view. She knew how passionate her youngest sister was about her work as a surgeon. 'Ashish is intelligent and has planned his career well—that is why he opted for an MD in medicine,' she said. 'He will get plenty of patients here. But you are an eye surgeon. How will you do any surgery here?' Sandhya reminded her sister how she would get upset when her professor would prefer another student to her to perform surgeries in college. 'Here you may get to perform cataract operations only on tigers,' Sandhya told her sister in jest.

It was the inherent goodness of the Renges that tilted the scales in favour of Ashish. The family decided that Ashish and Kavita would be a good match. The years have proven them right. 'She is way ahead of me in terms of service and devotion,' Ashish says about Kavita.

The weddings of the two other sons of Rambhau Satav were held with much pomp and grandeur. But when Ashish said he wanted to get married in a simple ceremony, it didn't surprise Rambhau at all. Ashish asked his father to give him the money that would otherwise be spent on his wedding, as he wanted to use it to build a critical care hospital in Melghat.

Kavita and Ashish got married in Akola on 30 November 1998 in a court ceremony. Ten family members represented both sides. Two days later, the couple left for Melghat.

~

Dr Kavita Satav arrived as a young bride to live in the hospital-cum-home in Dharni. The initial days of their married life were spent grappling with insects and reptiles. Snakes, scorpions and other creepy-crawlies were regular visitors to the house and the clinic. Tired of calling people to remove them, the couple learnt to do so themselves. Soon, they were adept at capturing even venomous snakes such as cobras.

The realization that this was what they were doing for the better part of most days troubled the doctor couple. Used to seeing nearly a hundred patients a day at the medical college, it was terribly boring and disheartening for the enthusiastic young doctors to sit idle with hardly any patient coming in.

The concept that there could be a special doctor to treat eye ailments was alien to the residents of Melghat then. In fact, they were not keen on visiting any kind of doctor for any treatment. The tribal people would prefer to consult a traditional healer from their community and believed in taking traditional medicines.

The 'treatment' they were used to was on the lines of voodoo, black magic and some locally grown herbs. They didn't even believe that Ashish and Kavita were doctors. It was beyond their comprehension that genuinely educated physicians would come from the city and live among them just to give them medical treatment.

Disease was all around. Deaths from preventable and treatable ailments such as pneumonia, diarrhoea and cerebral malaria happened almost every day. Malnutrition was the bane of the region, mostly stemming from the eating habits and lifestyle of the local tribes. All this added to the frustrations of the doctor couple. The locals were just not willing to visit hospitals or get themselves treated by doctors until it was too late for them to help.

One night, a man who had had a heart attack was admitted to the primary healthcare centre in Dharni. Since it was midnight and there was no doctor present, Ashish was called to treat him. The facility was horribly ill-equipped to handle such an emergency. There was no cardiac monitor or defibrillator; the closest critical care hospital was at least 150 kilometres away.

Ashish arrived at the hospital on his bicycle with an ECG machine, a bagful of medicines, and a big load of worries. In medical college, he had seen a team of three to four doctors treating an emergency patient, along with trained nurses in a well-equipped ICU. Here, all he had with him was an attendant who had studied up to Class VII. Ashish was also aware that if he started treatment and the patient died, the locals would lose all faith in him. He steeled his nerves, shut out the worries and began treatment. By early morning the patient was out of danger, and the doctor had cleared his first test with the locals.

After he treated another patient, comatose from brain haemorrhage, at his small hospital soon after, the people of Melghat accepted Ashish as a reliable doctor. Hospitals in Indore and Amravati had refused to admit the fifty-year-old patient, who had been brought back to Melghat. For seven days, Ashish remained at his bedside, constantly monitoring his condition and providing treatment. A crowd of some forty people parked themselves outside the hospital. When, on the eighth day, the patient could finally get up and walk, their faith in the doctor was cemented. It has never been shaken since.

~

However, though they kept hearing about people dying of various diseases in the villages, only a few would come to Ashish and Kavita for treatment. Determined to change that, Kavita one day decided that if the patients would not come, the doctors would go to them to provide treatment. Kavita and Ashish began journeying to the interior villages by bus to check on the ailing people. They trudged into the remotest corners, where buses would not go, on foot or in bullock carts. Many nights were spent under the open skies in the middle of deep forests.

On one such night after a hard day's work, the villagers had provided them with cots to sleep in the open. Ashish and Kavita knew that a tiger had been picking up cattle from the village regularly, and Kavita was petrified at the thought of encountering the beast. In the middle of the night, she woke up to sounds of something rustling near her. Then, Kavita could feel an animal against her feet. Scared to even move, she lay still for a while before screaming out. When they realized it was just a calf that was trying to settle in near her cot, nervous laughter followed all around.

Such outings, however, had to be curtailed when Kavita became pregnant. Three years after their marriage, on 1 May 2001, she gave birth to a son. The couple named him Athang, meaning 'endless'. He was born in Akola, and Kavita returned to Melghat with Athang when he was two months old.

Earlier the same year, Kavita had managed to set up an eye hospital in Dharni. However, it had not been able to attract any patients as the tribals were too poor to bear the cost of treatment. Kavita knew that there were many in the area who were suffering from various eye ailments and were not aware that their maladies could be cured with simple treatment. Kavita now decided to visit the villages and conduct door-to-door screening to identify patients.

Kavita could not leave Athang behind. She asked a local woman to fill in as a nanny. The three of them traversed across fifty villages to identify patients of cataract and other eye ailments. While Kavita attended to the patients, Athang would often sleep in a makeshift hammock. The nanny would take a bed sheet and tie its two ends to tree trunks. She would sit under a tree and keep a watchful eye on the boy, as the doctor checked the patients.

Ashish's family, aware of the hardships the couple faced, were keen to help. His elder brother gifted them an SUV because the family knew that Ashish and Kavita travelled by bullock cart to villages, and with an infant that would be even more fraught with trouble. Kavita, however, also used the vehicle to ferry patients to her hospital, where she would perform necessary surgeries and provide treatment. She would even prepare food for them—just like her mother did for strangers who came to the Akola nursing home for treatment.

Kavita's selfless service did not go unnoticed. Over time, the local people's faith in her became absolute; they knew they could turn to her for any emergency. One day, a family—Kavita had treated many of its members—requested her to assist with the delivery of a baby. Kavita told them she had no training in deliveries and that they should take the woman to a hospital. However, the family returned after three days. The baby had still not been born. They pleaded with her to come and help.

It was a difficult decision. Her first instinct was to say no. Ashish was attending to the OPD in Kolupur. Their hospital in Dharni was locked. Instruments required for the procedure were not available. However, her sense of duty prevailed over her reluctance and Kavita reached the home of the woman, carrying with her the equipment used for cataract surgeries.

It took all her medical acumen and practical skills—plus hours of hard work—to bring the baby into the world. As the women in the family announced that it was a boy, the family erupted in a celebration in the traditional style, by beating metal plates and banging on the doors. But the ordeal was not over for the doctor. Kavita was still struggling with the baby, who was yet to cry out.

Frantically, she began to pat him on the back, and gave him hot and cold water compresses. After a few minutes, the baby let out a feeble wail. That was enough to make the doctor hopeful. She realized that she needed to drain out the fluids that were choking the baby. Without wasting any more time, holding the infant close, she walked out of the home and looked around for some mode of transport to reach the hospital in Dharni. She found a rickety taxi that plied between the villages. As soon as she arrived at the hospital, Kavita asked for the suction machine. Only a manual one was available. She drained out the fluids and finally heard the baby's full-throated cries.

Once convinced that the infant was doing well, she brought him back to his home, only to discover that her work was still not over. The mother was in deep distress and was bleeding profusely. The dimming light of dusk was enveloping the room. There was, of course, no electricity. In torchlight, Kavita stitched up the woman. As she finished with the mother, she could hear the loud wails of the newborn. The baby was hungry. He needed to be fed. It was then that Kavita discovered that the mother also had lactation failure. She could not feed the child. Without his mother's milk the chances of the baby's survival were bleak.

The plight of the little boy she had brought into this world with such effort moved Kavita. All her efforts would come to naught if he were to die of hunger. Kavita, who had been nursing Athang, nursed the baby boy herself. For weeks she would send her own breast milk for the infant until he gained enough strength. That boy is now a strapping young man who never fails to acknowledge that had it not been for Kavita, he would not have lived.

~

Ashish and Kavita were walking more than the extra mile to ensure the local people got help, but their own moments of personal distress were filled with helplessness and nobody to turn to.

Their troubles began with Athang's innumerable bouts of illnesses.

On a cold night in December 2002, Ashish and Kavita woke up to the cries of their son, who was burning with high fever. Ashish began administering medicines for the fever but soon realized that the baby had abdominal pain. The flustered parents did not have the resources to shift the child to a hospital at 2 a.m. The difficult roads would make the journey dangerous, if not impossible. Athang's constant cries were piercing their hearts. Ashish decided to use his own clinical judgement. He changed medicines and the line of treatment. By morning, Athang was feeling better. But more setbacks were in store for them.

Soon after, Athang was afflicted with pneumonia. For a week his health showed no improvement—he did not respond to the treatment administered by his father. Melghat did not have a specialist or a paediatrician who could be consulted. Exasperated with his inability to treat the child, Ashish consulted paediatricians in Nagpur and Wardha. A change in medicines was advised and Athang was better after ten days.

The child's frequent illnesses were beginning to take a toll on the parents, who would stay awake night after night watching over him. The boy developed asthma at the age of three. The wet and cold climate of Melghat aggravated it.

Then came the ear-membrane rupture.

Ashish and Kavita, however, did not give up either on their work or on the well-being of their son. Athang's episodes of ill health ensured that Ashish studied medical books on paediatrics so that he could treat his son. This also led him to treat other children as patients.

When a widow brought her severely ailing child one night to his hospital soon after Athang's ear incident, Ashish thought of sending her to a city hospital. At the medical college, students are taught that it is always better to have a specialist treat a patient. But then Ashish remembered his own helplessness when his son had fallen ill. Turning away this woman and her child in the middle of the night would not be right. She had no means or resources to reach a hospital that was more than 150 kilometres away. Reading from books, Ashish pulled the child back from the brink of death.

The practice continued when a five-year-old girl suffering from cerebral malaria arrived at his hospital. She was having convulsions and Ashish realized that if the girl did not get treatment within half an hour, she would die. Just as he had helped ease his son's physical misery, he began treating her. After forty-eight hours, it was clear he had done it again. The child would live.

These successes gave a big boost to Ashish's confidence too.

The villagers began to trust the doctor couple, but getting hospitalized for diseases was still unfathomable to them. In spite of the help that the Satavs were extending, most tribals continued to prefer traditional healers, who do not have any formal education and rely on the information and knowledge passed from one generation of mendicants to another

One day, as Ashish was sitting outside his mud hut in Kolupur, which was his OPD, a woman arrived carrying her nine-year-old son. The boy was suffering from severe pneumonia. He had been treated so far by a quack. Feathers of birds were stuck on his chest, vermillion had been applied on his body and there were *damma*—burn marks—where he had been seared with a hot iron rod. His condition was critical.

The doctor told the mother that the child needed immediate hospitalization. The mother refused. 'I have three more children to take care of, there is a home to run, animals that have to be tended to,' she told him, leaving him speechless. 'What purpose will my going to a faraway hospital serve when I know that the child is already dying?'

Ashish was shocked. To him, a doctor from the city, it was unthinkable that a parent would give up on the treatment of their child. But the poor tribal woman's concerns lay with those back home who were still living. The child died after four days without any treatment. It left both Ashish and Kavita with a feeling of extreme inadequacy.

~

During the 1990s and most of the first decade of the new millennium, Melghat made news for its high child mortality rate. Children there were severely malnourished, and deaths from diarrhoea and pneumonia were common. Ashish and Kavita would regularly hear news of children dying in villages.

During the monsoon season in 2003, when five children died of diarrhoea in a single week in two villages, Kavita could not sleep for two nights. She kept her husband awake too. 'We are both doctors and yet such deaths are taking place regularly and so close to us, this is unbearable,' she told him in the middle of the night. 'Let us shut down our OPD and go out to the villages and treat children.'

Melghat has about 317 villages. Ashish was aware that there was no way that the two of them could reach out to each one of these villages and provide treatment. With great difficulty, he convinced his wife that mobile hospitals were not the answer. He promised to find a more practical solution.

Taking a leaf out of the practice followed by Dr Abhay Bang, Ashish, too, decided to build a team of barefoot doctors to reach the villages. He started training semi-literate tribal girls to identify and treat common paediatric illnesses. Once they were sufficiently trained, these healthcare workers fanned out across thirty-seven villages close to Dharni. They began to record the births and deaths of children and the diseases they suffered from. The exercise threw up inconvenient truths.

Though the government was spending a huge amount of money to fight malnourishment in Melghat, it was clear that the aid was not reaching the tribal people. The volunteers also found that government agencies were under-reporting deaths due to malnourishment. To put pressure on the state machinery, Ashish decided to go public with his findings.

He also realized why the tribal people were reluctant to go to hospitals—there was a severe communication gap between them and the government health apparatus. 'Doctors and health workers speak very differently from the dialects of local tribes,' Ashish explains.

If the tribal population was to be encouraged to bring their children and elders to the hospital, it was imperative that trust and a certain comfort level be created between them and the hospital staff. It was important that someone from their community be present at the hospital to serve as an intermediary between them and the hospital staff.

To that end, Ashish, who was also working with the government hospitals, began to explore ideas such as the appointment of tribal counsellors at state-run healthcare centres. His enthusiasm and initiatives, however, began to draw a lot of flak from the government hospital staff, local politicians and gram sabha members. Many did not want the status quo disturbed. Charges and complaints against Ashish began to fly thick and fast. It troubled

Ashish and Kavita, whose only concern was bettering the quality of healthcare being provided.

It would be counterproductive if locals were hostile to them, so Ashish decided that it would be more fruitful to focus on his dream project of building a critical care hospital—with the help that his father had promised at the time of his wedding.

With a loan from Rambhau, Ashish acquired a hectare of land in the middle of a forest. The construction of the hospital began in 2005, and Ashish's parents came down to Melghat to help him with the additional burden the project had put on him. In 2007, Ashish's dream of building a critical care hospital in Melghat came to fruition.

Located in the middle of nowhere, the hospital has been a boon for the people of Melghat. There are no wailing sirens of ambulances, screechy rolling of stretchers or the commotion of relatives of patients. What can be heard are mostly the reassuring beeps of health equipment and the low voice of the hospital's lone doctor as he moves from bed to bed, checking on the patients and issuing instructions to the six nurses who work with him.

Dr Ashish Satav is a powerhouse of energy. His bright eyes dart constantly from behind his thick spectacles, always vigilant. He takes calls almost every minute as he copes with the rush in the hospital, which thrives on aid from philanthropists from across the country and abroad. For the tribals, treatment is free.

The painstaking efforts of both Kavita and Ashish helped the tribals open up to modern medical treatment. They now came to the hospital with the belief that the two doctors can cure all ailments. From cancer to severe burns, the innocent villagers insist that the couple could and should treat them. 'I would get disturbed that we could not provide any relief to these patients who approached us with such hope,' Kavita remembers.

Woefully aware of the limitations they faced in the absence of specialists, general surgeons and anaesthetists, Kavita began to explore possibilities beyond Melghat. She deployed her networking skills and power of persuasion. 'I started calling up surgeons in hospitals in Nagpur to find out if they were willing to see a patient referred by me,' she says.

The good work the Satavs were doing in Melghat was known to the medical fraternity across Vidarbha. Doctors from across India, and even Australia, were more than willing to extend a helping hand. They offered treatment to those coming from Melghat—by physically seeing them or offering consultation through video calls.

However, there was still no solution in sight for those who required surgeries.

The critical care hospital built by the Satavs had a major and a minor operation theatre. It was now possible to perform surgeries there, but they needed surgeons. Ashish and Kavita reached out to doctors in the country and abroad to come and perform surgeries in Melghat. Scores of physicians, including plastic surgeons, orthopaedics, oncologists and anaesthetists, accepted their invitation.

The surgical camps, organized once or twice a year, tested not just the organizational skills of the Satavs but required all of the manpower at their disposal to work as a well-oiled unit. This included the entire family of Ashish. Both Rambhau and Kamal were present in Melghat whenever the camps were organized. Their work was to take care of the kitchen, where meals were cooked not just for the visitors but also for the patients and their attendants.

The Satavs' hospital in Dharni has since performed over a thousand surgeries. Expert physicians, eye surgeons and paediatricians have treated over a hundred thousand patients in the hospital. Nearly 22,000 patients have been treated in 317 speciality camps organized in Melghat.

The Satavs have run into rough weather along the way sometimes, but have never given up.

During an eye surgery camp in the early 2000s, a local man filed a case against them, accusing the doctor couple of hurling slurs about his caste. The charges were such that both Ashish and Kavita could have been arrested. Ashish was at the time planning to travel to Germany to present a research paper. Though used to facing such situations stoically, they were both rattled by the viciousness of the allegations.

Ashish suggested that Kavita shift the patients in the camp to a hospital in Amravati, but she refused to flinch. 'I will go ahead with the camp as the patients are all very old and at risk of losing their vision if not operated upon immediately,' she told him.

Her unshakable faith in God was her source of strength. She, however, also prepared for every eventuality. Athang's grandparents were there to take care of Athang in case Ashish and Kavita were arrested. 'If anybody speaks badly about your parents, tell them that my mother and father always support the truth,' Kavita told her son, who was just about five years old then.

Kavita's faith and the truth prevailed as the senior police officer who investigated the case found that the couple had made no derogatory remark.

Ashish, too, firmly believes in Gandhi's quote that 'truth can get troubled but it can never be defeated'. It is something the doctor lives by, and he says it has helped him overcome many difficult situations.

~

Dr Ashish and Dr Kavita Satav continue to work selflessly to reduce the pain and suffering of the community that they have adopted as their own. Their home, built adjacent to the hospital in Dharni, reflects their simple lifestyle. Devoid of any frills, the living room has a table at the centre that serves as a working desk and a dinner table. Both doctors are constantly in and out of their home, dividing their time between the hospital wards and the house. The kitchen is busy round the clock, as meals are prepared for patients, staff and guests.

'Our family is our biggest strength,' says Kavita. 'They have always supported us in everything and have made themselves available whenever we have required their help.'

Ashish's elder brother and his wife have now shifted to Melghat to help the doctors with some of the responsibilities.

The work that Ashish and Kavita have done and continue to do has been acknowledged by the country and, indeed, the world. In just eight years 'we could reduce by over 63 per cent the mortality rate of children under the age of five in sixteen villages', Ashish informs. The local administration decided to partner with him to implement his model of a home-based child care programme—in which trained volunteers go to homes to feed the babies the right nutrients—across Melghat.

Ashish's work showed that fighting malnutrition was key to bettering health indices, and that dietary changes were needed for the tribals. Helped by his grandfather, who was then in his late eighties, Ashish prepared a model of nutritional farms each measuring around half an acre. The locals were taught to cultivate green vegetables on this land. Vasantrao Bombatkar also reached Melghat to train the tribal population in farming.

Young Athang, too, has inherited his parents' high moral standards and unflinching spirit to serve the needy. He grew up with and studied in the same school as the tribal children of Melghat. He is naturally sensitive towards the underprivileged and reaches out to them. Once, when the family was waiting at Wardha station to board a train for Amravati, Athang, who was then in Class IX, spotted a young boy scavenging through the garbage piled near the tracks. He walked up to the boy and began chatting. The conversation continued until the train arrived. In that small moment, he had made a friend.

Athang has inherited his parents' knowledge as well, and is studying medicine from the college his mother graduated from. Ashish often feels the need for more doctors to come and work in Melghat. His woes could be coming to an end soon, for Athang plans to specialize in critical care.

About the Authors

Ashutosh Salil is a serving bureaucrat, a Maharashtra cadre IAS officer, who is also an alumnus of National Law School and Harvard Law School, and a Fulbright Scholar.

Barkha Mathur is an award-winning journalist from Nagpur, who has worked with leading news and media agencies for more than three decades and covered the stories of the people whose life and achievements appear in this book.